The Search for

THE UNDERGROUND

RAILROAD

— IN UPSTATE —

NEW YORK

The Search for

THE UNDERGROUND

RAILROAD

— IN UPSTATE —

NEW YORK

TOM CALARCO

THE
History
PRESS

Published by The History Press
Charleston, SC 29403
www.historypress.net

Copyright © 2014 by Tom Calarco
All rights reserved

Images from author's collection unless otherwise noted.

First published 2014

Manufactured in the United States

ISBN 978.1.62619.420.5

Library of Congress CIP data applied for.

CONTENTS

PREFACE

This book is about a journey that began in 1991 and "ended" in about 2002. However, it's still ongoing. It's the story of my connection to the history of the Underground Railroad and why I think it is such an important epoch in American history. I also consider the current state of studies regarding the Underground Railroad and suggest what we need to do to sort out the truth and arrive at a more accurate picture. It has been a labor of fascination and love, one that I will probably continue until I am no longer able. It is a story of a calling that I did not seek but which found me and brought meaning to my life.

Beginnings are always uncertain. You never know where things will lead, and you seldom realize that it's the beginning of something that could change your life. That's how it was when I was about to undertake a journey to learn the secrets withheld by the Underground Railroad, a journey that at times became an obsession.

I only had the vaguest notion of the Underground Railroad in 1991. I was doing a phone interview with a member of the Friends Meeting in Glens Falls, New York, about his church's history for the *Post-Star*, the local daily; I had been doing a series of church histories for the Sunday paper. The man claimed that his house had been a proverbial stop where fugitives from slavery were hidden. I don't recall if I even mentioned it in the eventual article. I did tell my editor, who asked to see what I could dig up about the local Underground Railroad.

I discovered more than I had expected. An oral tradition, based mainly on the 1927 memoir of an eighty-four-year-old man named Samuel Boyd, revealed stories about his father's participation and an unforgettable firsthand account. One summer morning in 1851, while eight-year-old Boyd and nine-year-old Add Stoddard were roller-skating, a man got off a stagecoach and asked them where he could find the barber John Van Pelt. "'Oh, yes,' [Boyd] said, and started to show him when Add roughly brushed [him] aside, and said, 'He don't know where he lives. I will show you.'"

To Boyd's surprise, Stoddard sent him in the wrong direction. Stoddard had learned from his father that slave hunters might be looking for Van Pelt's fugitive slave wife. The couple had three children. Stoddard then went to his father, chiropractor Joseph Stoddard, and in less than an hour, the Van Pelt family was on their way to Canada.[1] After settling them in Prescott, Canada, just across the St. Lawrence River from Ogdensburg, Van Pelt returned to Glens Falls. Selling his barbershop, he rejoined them in Canada.[2]

Boyd also recalled another incident. One winter morning in the barn, while feeding their cow, he heard someone snoring and saw a pair of shoes sticking out from a pile of hay. He ran out and told his father, Rufus, who told him to calm down. "You are not to say a word about this to anyone," his father ordered. Twice that day, he saw his father take food in a pail to the barn. When night fell, his father loaded their sleigh, hitched up the horses and left with the mysterious man on a three-day trip. During that time, his mother explained everything to him. His father was taking two fugitives from slavery to Swanton, Vermont, where they would be conveyed to Canada. What impressed him was the absolute secrecy about this, and Boyd wrote that he never told anyone about it until after the Civil War.[3]

Chestertown historian Jane Parrott was my most knowledgeable informant at the time. A kindly woman, typical of many other local historians I would meet who would do anything to help your research, she was the carrier of the oral legends of her local Underground Railroad, like many other historians throughout the United States. She welcomed me into her spacious nineteenth-century home that was once a temperance tavern in her sleepy village at the gateway to the Adirondack Mountains. Surrounded by small mountains thick with evergreen, Chestertown is an inviting place in the summer, but its winters require woodstoves to work overtime.

She took me into her living room and showed me a letter. It was written by Emily McMasters, who had formerly been the curator of the Clinton County Historical Association, just to the north. According to the letter, Reverend Thomas Baker of the former Darrowsville Church a few miles down the road from Chestertown

Chestertown in the nineteenth century. *Courtesy Phyllis Bogle, Town of Chester historian.*

used to help John Brown aid fugitives from slavery. The letter also quoted from the diary of Lucia Newell Oliver, who claimed that her stepfather, Reverend Enos Putnam of nearby Johnsburg, aided fugitives from slavery: "I came down the stairs in my nightgown. Father was just opening the cellar door. He had a lighted candle in one hand and a plate of food in the other. He did not see me and I followed him part way down the cellar stairs. He set the plate of food on a box and unlocked the door of a room in the cellar where mother kept her preserves. I could see from my perch, two or three steps down that there was a kind of bed in the room and a young man, very black, sat on it. I was frightened for I had never seen a black man before and I hurried to go back to bed."[4]

Parrott also said that Chestertown resident Joseph Leggett aided fugitives from slavery, a story that had been passed down through the family, who still owned the old house. Like the Darrowsville Church (which had long been abandoned), the Leggett House was located south of Chestertown. It was a short ride down Route 9, the main street of Chestertown, to the home, a typical white Georgian-style country home with shutters. It looked like no one was living there, although it appeared to be in fine condition. The church, however, was not. It was only a shell of a structure.[5]

Ten miles south of Chestertown, along Route 9, Warrensburg historian Mabel Tucker told me about tunnels that were found connecting two nineteenth-century houses, one a nicely kept white Greek Revival house on

Old Darrowsville Church.

130 Main Street with a white picket fence and the other the senior citizens' center, suggesting to her the possibility that they might have been used for the Underground Railroad. Fifteen miles farther down Route 9 in South Glens Falls, just across the Hudson River from the home of Samuel Boyd, two more houses had oral traditions suggesting involvement in the Underground Railroad. One was the office of the Moreau Historical Society, which had a trapdoor that led to a five- by ten-foot crawl space separated from its cellar. The other had been the home of Reverend John Folsom, one of the founders of the First Presbyterian Church in Glens Falls. Slave shackles had been found in the cellar of this house. A former owner of the house, William Connelly, told me that he was sure the house had been a stop not only because of the stories passed down but also because of evidence of tunnels, now blocked off, that led to the river.

At the time, I thought it reasonable to suggest that evidence of a tunnel was persuasive. However, I later found that this meant little and needed to be considered along with many other factors. In fact, I would discover that serious historians ridiculed any mention of a tunnel and considered it a red flag as to a location's authenticity.

Six miles farther south was the Gansevoort mansion, built by the son of Revolutionary War general Peter Gansevoort. Moreau historian Margery Sexton said that it had been owned by her sister and pointed to a large space between the house's two fireplaces as a possible hideaway. She referred me to Bernard Shaw, a man who had lived in the area since 1920. He remembered hearing stories as a boy from black families about fugitives from slavery who didn't go all the way to Canada and settled in Gansevoort. Another historian, Georgia Ball, said that the Gansevoorts had slaves until the 1827 state law outlawed the "peculiar institution"; they remained to work for them because of their loyalty. Their presence, she suggested, may have made the mansion a possible destination for fugitives from slavery.

These were the stories I collected in Warren and northern Saratoga County. None of them had any written documentation except for Boyd's personal memoir and the brief notes left behind by the son of Joseph Leggett. All of the others, though, were associated with hidden spaces or tunnels. Remember this for future reference.

In neighboring Washington County, another writer, Hope Ferguson, collected more oral stories, and the newspaper editor combined our collections into one long feature that was the front-page headline story for the Sunday edition. It aroused a great deal of local interest, and we were invited to speak at the Chapman Museum as part of its Civil War roundtable series. I had never met Hope, and our meeting resulted in a long friendship. I'll never forget the first time she invited me to her home in a remote section of Washington County and showed me a picture of her father and mother with President and Mrs. Kennedy. Her father had been the ambassador to Nigeria during the Kennedy administration, and she had lived in Africa during her childhood. Her parents had since passed, but her aunt, who had published a few novels, lived nearby.

The irony of the invitation was that neither Hope nor I knew much about the Underground Railroad other than the stories we had collected. So, we spent the next month preparing our presentation. I don't even recall all the books we read. I believe one of the first I read was Wilbur Siebert's classic *The Underground Railroad: From Slavery to Freedom*, published in 1898. I also read, for the first time, *Twelve Years a Slave*, the story of Solomon Northup, who had been kidnapped in nearby Saratoga; the work was well known to historians in our area. The Siebert book, though, was by far the most important. It

Riding the Underground Railroad

By Tom Calarco and Hope Ferguson
Correspondents

It's midnight and you're walking, with nature buzzing all around you. The hills are beginning to open, and a valley is supposed to be coming up. Your only guide is the North Star as you seek a house with big pillars, the home of a "conductor."

The year is 1850, and you're a runaway slave, running toward Canada and freedom, with only the longing in your heart and the kindness of strangers to sustain you.

In 1793, Congress passed the Fugitive Slave Act, providing for the seizure of slaves who had run away from their masters. In response to ever more strident Southern demands, the Fugitive Slave Act of 1850 was passed, making it illegal for anyone to help runaway slaves.

Hiram Corliss was born in Easton the same year the first Fugitive Slave Act was approved. An influential surgeon, writer and proprietor of a general store, Corliss was also an avid abolitionist. His two houses in Union (now Greenwich) were important stops on the Underground Railroad, the house was later converted into the Central House Hotel, the other still stands on Bridge Street.

Corliss also was at view with the feelings of quite a few people in the North Country. The Friends Meeting House in North Easton, for instance, hosted anti-slavery meetings with such well-known aboli-

tionist speakers as Lucretia Mott and Sojourner Truth, a black woman who returned to the South many times to bring others to freedom.

From the peace-loving Quakers who founded Easton and Glens Falls to the militant John Brown in North Elba, the feeling that slavery should be abolished was widespread. And many people acted on those feelings by serving as Underground Railroad "conductors."

Though not truly underground nor a railroad, the term fit well for the escape route used by runaway slaves, for the proceedings necessarily were secret, and runaways stopped at many "stations" on their journeys north.

The fact that the conductors were secretive allowed them to operate with relative impunity, but it has bedeviled local historians trying to trace the routes. A few letters, a diary entry or two, and hidden rooms and passageways that may — or may not — have been part of the railroad are the only hard evidence that a particular house was part of the route.

Washington County and Argyle historian Doris McEachron has one document pertaining to the railroad, a research paper written in 1959 by a student, Jesse Williams, attempting to follow the trail through this area. Williams speculated the railroad followed the "old Coach Road" from Troy, running north

See Freedom: Page A6

Stops Along the Underground Railroad

Darrowsville

Abolitionist minister Thomas Baker and the congregation of the Wesleyan-Methodist church made Darrowsville a station.

South Glens Falls

The Rice or Folsom House, next to the McDonald's in South Glens Falls used to have tunnels that led to the river.

WARREN COUNTY
WASHINGTON COUNTY
SARATOGA COUNTY

Argyle

This brick home is currently owned by James Dier, Main Street, Argyle. Tunnels were found in the cellar during a routine cleaning.

Greenwich

This house on the corner of Main and Academy in Greenwich is the former home of Leonard Gibbs, an abolitionist involved with the railroad. It is now a chiropractor's office.

Railroad's history still a mystery

"Who laid the Underground Railroad? Perhaps a Paul Bunyan equipped with a frontier magic scooped up the earth with his fist and shot out his arm in tunnels north and south in the land ... or perhaps trails vaporized behind runaways by some sort of voodoo magic."

So begins "Let My People Go," Henrietta Buckmaster's account of the Underground Railroad. Mystification, she wrote, was essential to the operation of the "railroad," so outlandish tales of how fugitive slaves managed to be spirited away without a trace proliferated throughout the life of the escape route.

The trail of the Underground Railroad has long been cold, but even now, an air of mystery hangs over its operation. Even in towns that are historically known to have hosted passengers on their way to the "promised land" — Canada — the exact extent and location of many of the stations has been lost by the passage of time.

Because the need for secrecy was so great, many records, including letters, were systemati-

Because the need for secrecy was so great, many records, including letters, were systematically destroyed by the participants.

cally destroyed by the participants. There's also a great deal of disagreement about how many slaves escaped north; the Encyclopaedia Britannica says estimates vary from 40,000 and 100,000.

Though rumors fly about homes that may have been stations, and about secret rooms in attics, cellars and beneath floors, there is no consensus about how extensive the railroad was in this area among local historians.

Hartford historian Sylvia Van Anden cautioned against unsubstantiated tales. She said she knows of no homes in Hartford, for instance, that were definitely used by the railroad.

At one time she investigated a house in South Hartford, the "McCoy property," which was

rumored to have a secret room in the cellar. The elderly woman who responded to her questions told Van Anden it was a milk room, and the historian had no reason to dispute that.

But in another Hartford farmhouse, a real estate agent showed a potential buyer two secret rooms — one off a bedroom that could be entered only through a narrow cupboard door, and another hidden beneath the carpeting in the living room.

"One had no window," said Colleen Bolden. "You'd have to crawl through the cupboard door to get into it."

She was told by the real estate agent that it was a maid's quarters. But Bolden had definite ideas and differing — feelings about the rooms real purpose.

"In school I was taught about the Underground Railroad," she said. "The rooms made me think of it because they were so obviously hidden. If (one) was a maid's quarters, why didn't it have a door, or why didn't they have windows?"

Glens Falls *Post-Star*, March 10, 1991.

probably is the most comprehensive book about the Underground Railroad ever written. A history professor at Ohio State University, Siebert gathered much of his information from the accounts of still-living participants in the Underground Railroad or their surviving family members. In recent years, a number of contemporary interpreters of the Underground Railroad have criticized Siebert and his method, claiming that many of those accounts were exaggerated. This has become for me a pivotal issue in determining the truth about the Underground Railroad, one that I will cover in more detail later.

To our surprise, the lecture room of the Chapman was standing room only. I have given many presentations since, and it was the only time I have presented before an overflowing crowd. The audience received us enthusiastically and asked many questions, including some that we couldn't answer. The occasion left a lasting impression on me. There was something special about the Underground Railroad that had turned it into a legend.

The friendship between Hope and I bloomed, and we continued to do research about the Underground Railroad, mainly in Washington County, which was mostly farm country and which I found to be much more active than Warren County. We continued to collect information, but after some time, the passion waned as we both had other writing interests. A few years later, my peripatetic lifestyle led me to Ithaca, New York.

I had lived in Ithaca a decade earlier, when I was pursuing fiction writing, and I had befriended Cornell poet A.R. Ammons and novelist Lamar Herrin. At the *Post-Star* and later the *Chronicle*, the Glens Falls weekly that focused on the arts, I had been regularly covering arts events and reviewing concerts, mainly classical music, which was especially active during the summer months in the Adirondacks. In Ithaca, I picked up a job covering arts for the weekly insert of the *Ithaca Journal*. I don't recall how I got wind of the Underground Railroad in Ithaca. I believe someone told me that Harriet Tubman had been a member of one of the local churches there. It revived what had been a flagging interest.

I went to the Cornell library, or I should say Olin, the main library, because Cornell has about twenty libraries. Searching the card catalogue—this was 1993, the days before everything was on computer—I found an interesting entry: a bachelor's thesis written by Elbert C. Wixom in 1903. It turned out that Wixom's grandfather had been part of the Underground Railroad. Wixom also had interviewed still-living participants. His thesis reported their accounts and included a blueprint of a map, from which I created the sketch shown on page 14.

I soon found a large number of historical references and accounts about abolitionism in Ithaca—this combination of Quakers in the surrounding countryside along with black barbers and ministers, as well as disgruntled Presbyterians who disagreed with their church's failure to oppose slavery, formed the core of the local Underground Railroad. The *Ithaca Journal* published my account and helped me create my first of many Underground Railroad maps.

Perhaps the most active local conductor was George Johnson, a fugitive slave from Georgia who set up a barbershop in the basement of the Ithaca Hotel on North Aurora Street. In several interviews given around the turn of the century, Johnson's son, George, testified to his own dealings regarding fugitives from slavery with Ithaca mayor Ben Johnson.[6] According to George, he and his father aided 114 fugitives from slavery during their years of participation.[7] Even before Johnson, an Underground station existed in Ithaca. Emma Galvin's 1941 thesis, which I also found at Olin, identified its location at least as early as 1824 at 326 South Cayuga Street, where a black man named Titus Brum lived. According to the lore, fugitives were hidden there in a space behind the oven.[8]

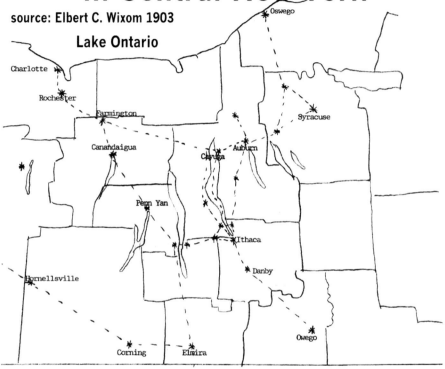

Some Stops Along the Underground Railroad in Central New York

source: Elbert C. Wixom 1903

Lake Ontario

Oswego
Charlotte
Rochester
Farmington
Syracuse
Canandaigua
Auburn
Cayuga
Penn Yan
Ithaca
Danby
Hornellsville
Owego
Corning
Elmira

Central New York Underground Railroad. *Courtesy Elbert C. Wixom, 1903.*

Opposite: *Ithaca Journal,* February 1993.

In these early days, blacks were the primary agents. Many were former fugitives from slavery. In about 1825, local blacks organized St. James African Methodist Episcopal Zion Church, a focal point of local Underground activity. In 1836, they built the church that still stands on Cleveland Avenue and where Harriet Tubman visited on her journeys bringing slaves to freedom. Not only were Titus Brum and George Johnson members, but the white mayor, Ben Johnson, sang in the church choir as well. Another

Stops on the Underground Railroad

Some of the links in a chain of 'Stations' have been traced in Tompkins County

By TOM CALARCO
Special to The Journal

IF you were a runaway slave during the 1850s, Ithaca might have seemed like the Promised Land. Though the city had its share of anti-abolitionists as did most Northern towns, it also had a committed contingent of white abolitionists and black freemen who worked together to help fugitives to freedom.

The usual route brought fugitives via Montrose, Pa. and Owego. A turnpike existed then linking Owego with "the Forest City" as Ithaca was once known. Along the way, a fugitive might've stopped in Danby at the farm of Doctor Louis Beers, whose home had secret rooms to hide fugitives. The good Doctor would then take them into town by wagon.

A focal point of Underground Railroad activity in Ithaca was St. James African Methodist Episcopal Zion Church, a mostly black congregation, on Wheat St. now Cleveland Ave. Its building erected in 1836 still stands as the oldest church in the city and outside it a plaque commemorates its role in the Underground Railroad.

Not only did the church assist the loosely organized group of Underground members in town, but it also served as a stopover for many of the legendary Harriet Tubman's 19 journeys during which she led over 300 slaves to freedom. At least four slaves whom "Aunt Harriet" helped to freedom settled in Ithaca: Tom Allen, Jasper Woodson, Jerry Jones, and a Miss Hattie. Documents testifying to this are preserved in the Harriet Tubman Museum in Auburn, said Rev. Cyril Larmond, current pastor of St. James.

But even before the existence of St. James, the oldest known central New York station was located in 1824 at 76 S. Cayuga (now somewhere between 326 and 330 S. Cayuga). There has been some confusion about the location of this stop among researchers because the city's street numbers were changed in the 1890s. In any case, an 1866 map of Ithaca shows it to be the third house on the west side of Cayuga St. north of Six Mile Creek.

This early Station was the home of agent Francis Bloodgood who later sold it to a free black named Titus Brum. It may have even seen more active than the church, for Brum was the father-in-law of Ithaca's best known conductor, George Johnson.

Johnson was a fugitive from Georgia who set up a barber shop in the basement of the Ithaca Hotel on the corner of Aurora and Owego St. now State St. He is reputed to have personally helped 114 fugitives to freedom. In he Thomas Borns book, "Initial Ithacans," published in 1903, Johnson's son (also named George) related his father's Underground association with Ben Johnson, a prominent lawyer and former "President" (the early term or mayor) of Ithaca.

"Occasionally I visited Mr. Johnson in his office and informed him that several runaway slaves had arrived during the previous night by way of the 'underground route,' and that they must have shoes and clothing and money for heir passage to Canada . . . he would hand me a five or ten dollar bill note, and tell me to

take it and buy tickets, and send the runaways back to their masters. He knew that [they] would be . . . secreted during the night in the steamboat 'Simeon DeWitt' and taken to Cayuga Bridge and on toward the North Star."

In another interview that same year, the younger Johnson outlined the local operation of the Underground for Cornell student Elbert Wixom, whose 1903 thesis about the region's Underground Railroad is stored at the university.

"During the boating season," he told

Wixom, "they were concealed in the hold of steamers and taken direct to Cayuga, where they joined the main line . . . and to Rochester and Charlotte. Occasionally one would go east and reach the lake at Oswego."

But if the boats were not running, Johnson said, the fugitives were forced to go overland. Stops existed on both sides of the lake. Two miles northwest of Ithaca, Deacons Hoyt and Luce ran a church which still stands near the Frear Cemetery and which sheltered and fed

See STOPS, 6B

A 'STATION' ON THE RAILROAD: *The Parker-Wixom House on Buck Hill Road in Mecklenburg as it stands today.*
HEATHER MARTIN/Journal Staff

Journal map

Conductors, stations, and 'hidey-holes'

By TOM CALARCO
Special to The Journal

The story of the Underground Railroad, a secret but intricate network that led slaves to freedom prior to the Civil War, is among the most honorable chapters in our nation's history.

Its origins probably go back to 1775 when the first anti-slavery society was founded by Quakers in Philadelphia. Historians point to a 1786 letter written by George Washington about a runaway slave indicating an organization had formed in Philadelphia to help such fugitives.

However, until after 1830 such activities were sporadic. By that time slavery had been outlawed in states north of the Mason-Dixon line and the Abolitionist movement had begun to pick up steam. Because of its illegal nature — those convicted of breaking the Fugitive Slave Law were liable to huge fines and prison terms — the Underground Railroad left few written records and never became a formal organization. It did evolve, however, into a far reaching network and adopted terminology from the railroad, the technological wonder of the age. Stations

See CONDUCTORS, 6B

source, an 1889 letter to the *Ithaca Journal* from Edward S. Esty, noted that the coordinator of the local Underground Railroad was the pastor of Zion's church.[9] The brother of Esty was a mayor of Ithaca, and he also confessed to being part of the local Underground Railroad, as did Alexander Murdoch, who made a similar confession in a letter to the *Journal* and whose house on 33 South Geneva Street was threatened with destruction by a mob because of his activities.

Around 1837, a conflict over the slavery question arose locally in the First Presbyterian Church regarding the failure of its pastor to condemn the laws protecting slavery. Its leading member, Benjamin S. Halsey, was identified by Johnson as being involved in the Underground Railroad, as was another Presbyterian, banker Josiah B. Williams, who allegedly hid fugitives from slavery in the basement of his bank at 214 West State Street. Another member of the church's abolitionists, Charles Hayt, formed his own congregation north of the city along Cayuga Lake on the present Route 79. This church, Johnson said, also harbored fugitives from slavery. In the 1850s, divisiveness over slavery decreased, and this was the period when Harriet Tubman was regularly welcomed by locals to rest and refresh herself with her parties of slaves fleeing to Canada for freedom. Occasionally, some stayed in Ithaca and became permanent residents, like Tom Allen, Jasper Woodson, Jerry Jones and Miss Hattie.

Elbert Wixom also interviewed George Johnson. "During the boating season," he told Wixom, "they were concealed in the hold of steamers and taken directly to Cayuga, where they joined the main line…and to Rochester and Charlotte. Occasionally one would go east and reach the lake at Oswego… But if the boats were not running, the fugitives were forced to go overland."[10]

Another part of the local network was the Carman/Wixom residence on Buck Hill Road outside Mecklenberg. Elbert Wixom wrote that a ferry operated by his ancestor William Carman took fugitives from Ludlowville to Trumansburg.

According to Mary Lou Van Buren, the 1993 owner of the Wixom family house on Buck Hill Road between Ithaca and Trumansburg, the house had "a hidden room of about fifty square feet." Another local researcher, whose name and article I cannot recall, though it's somewhat inconsequential, reported that as many as one thousand fugitives from slavery may have been aided in the Ithaca area from 1830 to 1860.

Once again, the story of the hidden rooms was reported, and the figure of one thousand regarding the number of fugitives from slavery who were aided was alleged. I later found that this round figure was commonly associated with conductors and their involvement in the Underground Railroad. The problem with such estimates is that they're based on complete and utter speculation without a shred of evidence.

The Ithaca research was fun and put together an interesting picture. However, it was very cursory, and my involvement in studying the Underground Railroad was put on the back burner for the next several years, waiting for the moment it would be rekindled.

Chapter 1

QUAKER COUNTRY

In 1995, a committee of noted historians, chaired by well-known Underground Railroad history promoter Charles Blockson and which had been commissioned by the National Park Service, recommended that a national effort be devoted to stress the significance of the Underground Railroad and to recover and preserve its history before it was lost.

I don't recall exactly when I heard about this. I think it was from my friend, the late Sweet Mama Stringbean herself, Shirley McFerson. She was the longtime director of the Caldwell Library in Lake George, New York, and we had met in writing groups more than a decade earlier. I can still hear her raucous laughter and fondly recall her upbeat character that drew her to roles in local theater, wearing outlandish costumes and taking on whimsical personas, like Sweet Mama Stringbean, for the storytelling she did for children.

By this time, I had moved back from Ithaca and resumed my role as an arts writer and music reviewer for the *Chronicle*. The news of the report piqued my interest, and while researching possible markets for freelance articles, I saw that *Cobblestone*, the history magazine for kids, was doing an issue on the abolition of slavery. I submitted an idea about the role of the Quakers, and it was accepted. Embedded in the article were two paragraphs about the Quakers in Easton, Washington County. Not long after it was published, I received a call from the Easton Public Library, asking if I would come to the library and talk about the Underground Railroad. I was hesitant. The only thing I knew about that community

Wilbur Farmhouse in Easton.

were those two paragraphs. But I agreed to come and talk about it with the director of the library, Helen Brownell.

The truth never changes, only our perception of it. Likewise for history. For me, the Underground Railroad was still this huge mystery about which we knew very little. It was the summer of 1996, and I was driving through the town of Easton, New York, along Route 40, where the old Coach Road once crossed through the same rolling farmland toward green foothills, countryside that Grandma Moses painted. Nothing distinguishes it from countless other rural places in America except that 160 years ago, it was one of those havens for people seeking freedom. And like many such places, it was a Quaker community.

Our meeting was a revelation because Helen knew a lot more about Easton's Underground Railroad than I did. The late Oren B. Wilbur had left behind stories about his grandparents' role that the local historical society had published thirty years earlier. Oral tradition identified other "stops," and I suggested that we apply for a grant to do a joint study involving the Easton community. She agreed to help write the grant and organize the community. After a local arts organization funded us, a deadline was set and the fun began.

Samuel Cornish, founder of the *Colored American* and one of the founders of the New York Committee of Vigilance.

Some antislavery newspapers.

The locals were equally enthusiastic, and they gathered family lore and told me that such and such house was used or that there was another house that had burned down or another that had been demolished. My most important lead came from someone outside the community: the respected Quaker historian Chris Densmore, then the archivist at the University of Buffalo and currently at Swarthmore College, outside Philadelphia. I had received his contact information from an Easton resident. I wrote to him, and he advised me to search the abolitionist newspapers of the day. He also said that there was an index to these newspapers, *Anti-Slavery Newspapers and Periodicals*, edited by abolitionist scholar John Blassingame, that had been completed in 1984.

Thirty miles south, the New York State Library in Albany held a copy. That first day at the library, I found that it consisted of five thick hardcover volumes. Now began the work of looking for reports of Wilburs and others who were part of oral Underground Railroad lore in Washington County in the newspapers of that time. These would be primary documents, in many cases the most reliable sources. Until that time, we had mainly secondary sources for our information about the local Underground Railroad—for example, the *History of Greenwich* by Elisha P. Thurston, published in 1876, and the *History of Greenwich* by Mrs. B.F. Sharpe, published in 1909. Probably the most authoritative documents were an April 22, 1858 article about a visit from slave catchers in Grant J. Tefft's *The Story of Union Village* and the papers of Oren B. Wilbur.

My efforts soon hit pay dirt, and like any miner who finds gold, my search intensified. I found letters and reports written by local abolitionists Dr. Hiram Corliss, Erastus Culver and Leonard Gibbs. One especially remarkable document came from the *Pennsylvania Freeman* in 1839, a detailed account by noted abolitionist and then president of the New York Anti-Slavery Society Henry B. Stanton of an antislavery convention in Union Village (the antebellum name of Greenwich), which is about seven miles from Easton.

The account reported that among those who attended were national antislavery leaders with whom I was unfamiliar at that time: Gerrit Smith, Joshua Leavitt, Luther Lee and William L. Chaplin, as well as Nathaniel Colver and Erastus Culver, locals who would become nationally prominent abolitionists. The convention passed a strong resolution "to aid in the escape of fugitives from slavery," and Stanton added, "Great interest was felt on this topic…and, unless I greatly misread the signs of the times, the day is approaching when it will be…impossible for the despots of the South to carry the panting fugitives back to chains from central and northern New York."[11]

Another was an account in *The Liberator* by Dr. Corliss about an 1854 visit of Frederick Douglass and his lectures in Galeville, Lakeville, Shushan, Cambridge, Union Village and at the South Meetinghouse in Easton. "The impression on the minds of the people, by his meetings, was very good indeed," Corliss wrote. "Those I heard were full of great truths, sound logic, and enforced by vivid illustrations, and entirely free from all cant or slang."[12]

Wilbur Farmhouse.

These and other accounts that I continued to find reinforced the legendary stories supplied by Oren Wilbur. One of his stories concerned a fugitive slave who had been tracked down by slave catchers during the early 1850s to Job and Esther Wilbur's farmhouse, which remains much as it was 160 years ago:

> *He was in the house but a short time when they heard the pursuers coming down the lane…The poor fugitive was hustled up into the garret by means of a ladder and trap door. On the way through the dining room, the slave saw on the table a long carving knife which he grabbed as he went along, but his hosts, being Friends, and in favor of nonviolence objected; but the colored man insisted that he was not going to be taken alive… By this time, the two men had arrived at the house, and…demanded where the slave was. Of course Job and Esther gave them no information; but by the authority of The Fugitive Slave Law, they went ahead and searched the house. Not finding him but seeing the ladder leading up to the garret, one of the men climbed up it and stuck his head through the trap door. There stood the slave, knife in hand, and threatened to use it if the man came any further. After parleying awhile and seeing the slave was*

desperately in earnest, he came down and the two went away to secure more help…

As soon as they were gone…Job hitched a horse to the carriage, while Esther dressed the man up in her clothes including a thick veil inside her Quaker bonnet and soon the slave was his way to Union Village, to the home of Dr. Hiram Corliss, the next station of the Underground Railroad.[13]

Another episode recounted by Oren Wilbur told of Esther Wilbur opening the meetinghouse in North Easton (there were two meetinghouses in Easton), where antislavery meetings had been forbidden:

At one time, an Anti-Slavery meeting was appointed to be held in the meeting house in the afternoon following a mid-week meeting…John Wilbur, Jr. [Job Wilbur's cousin] was caretaker of the house…and not being in sympathy with the Anti-Slavery movement, decided not to allow the house to be opened for the occasion. After the morning meeting had closed…Esther still remained seated. John Jr. waited a little while then went to her and said, "Esther, I want to close the meeting house now and thee will have to go." Esther still remained seated but replied "John, thee can lock up the meeting house, but I have not finished my worship so want to stay a little while longer." After several attempts to persuade her, he locked the doors and went home. The door on the woman's side of the house was buttoned on the inside, so when it came time for the afternoon meeting, Esther simply unbuttoned the door and the people came in and held their meeting as planned. John Wilbur, Jr. accepted his defeat and ever after the North Easton Friend meeting house was open to any Anti-Slavery meeting that wished to use it.[14]

To corroborate this story, Helen found an 1853 letter reporting that the North Meetinghouse was also the site of lectures by Sojourner Truth and Lucretia Mott. I also found her obituary in the *National Antislavery Standard*. In part, it said:

She was one of the earliest to espouse the anti-slavery cause; and although possessed of but a frail physical organization, yet no one in this country has rendered that hated cause more efficient service…Through her efforts mainly (although actively opposed by prominent members of that meeting) the Friends meeting-house at North Easton was first opened to anti-slavery meetings, some eight or ten years since, and from that time its doors have been kept open to the anti-slavery laborer.[15]

Finally, our study was concluded, and I wrote a paper detailing our findings that was submitted to the funding organization, as required. The study was finalized with a presentation at the library during which I read the papers and those in the community reported their contributions. It was a great success, and like my earlier presentation at the Chapman Museum, the enthusiasm of the community reinforced my confidence and pushed me along the road of Underground Railroad research. I was discovering that just because the Underground Railroad was secret and nothing was written down, this didn't mean that its mysteries could never be revealed. I sensed that there were mountains of evidence. It just needed hard work to dig it out, and I was determined to do it.

Chapter 2

THE FREE CHURCH

Six years had passed since I wrote that first Underground Railroad article. I was hooked but not obsessed, at least not yet. I was finding that the real heart of the area's Underground Railroad was Union Village. However, I began to encounter some resistance, notably from Helen Hoag, a historian who had researched the village's history for many years. She and others cautioned that so little had been written down that my efforts would be futile.

I tried to explain to them that I already had made some revealing discoveries, but they refused to listen. In addition to the Blassingame *Index*, I had learned that a project to microfilm old newspapers throughout the state had recently been completed and that many of the newspapers were available at the New York State Library. I began spending all my free time there and with good reason. I was making one new find after another.

Believe me, if you like history, unearthing forgotten stories can be exhilarating. You become immersed in the microfilm and neglected archives, and you find ephemeral treasures among the crumbling pages of rare newspapers. You also feel as if you are visiting the past, your thoughts dwelling in another time. It makes you appreciate those from the past, and you begin to have private conversations with them; they become like departed friends and relatives you will always revere. Well, maybe I already was obsessed.

Nevertheless, my success in Easton led to my being subsidized by two grants from Furthermore in Hudson, New York, with the obligation to produce a book based on my research. Not nearly enough to live on—maybe

The Orthodox Congregational "Free" Church.

enough to pay for gas for the hundreds of trips I made to the state library during the next seven years. Although it took that long to produce the first book, it did happen. But I had a long way to go.

At the time, I was still pretty naïve about the Underground Railroad. Wilbur Siebert's book was my bible. For me, the Underground Railroad was the story of good Samaritans helping their fellow brothers and sisters along various routes to freedom. Siebert later published books that covered the Underground Railroad in Vermont, Massachusetts and Ohio. His findings were based primarily on thousands of responses to inquiries he made of those who participated in the Underground Railroad or their relatives and friends; he began circulating these responses in 1892.

For many years, information about the Underground Railroad originated mainly from such recollections. Siebert's collection was part of a body of work of remembrances of the Underground Railroad published mainly in the nineteenth century. Most notable were William Still's *The Underground Railroad: A Record*, Levi Coffin's *Reminiscences* and Robert Smedley's *History of the Underground Railroad in Chester County, Pennsylvania*. All presented a story of a loosely organized network of individuals who, through various means, aided tens of thousands of slaves obtain their freedom, with many being sent to Canada.

I was unaware of the criticism of Siebert's work and of the contempt among academics for the popular notions of hidden rooms and tunnels, as well as other fanciful trappings like the use of quilts. This perspective was first given serious currency by Larry Gara's book, *Liberty Line*, published in 1961. Gara argued that there was little organization in the Underground Railroad, that the number of fugitives from slavery aided had been exaggerated by propaganda and that the role played by blacks was underemphasized.[16] A later, more radical position on the self-promotion of white abolitionists was taken by the prominent academic David Blight, who said that Siebert's sources were polluted by "sentimental retrospection."[17]

I don't recall the first time I read Gara's book. When I did, I readily accepted some of his tenets, especially the one about the role of blacks in the Underground Railroad. In my later book *People of the Underground Railroad*, I profiled one hundred individuals who made important contributions. The breakdown by race was sixty-one white and thirty-nine black individuals. I acknowledge that blacks were more likely to assist fugitives from slavery. At the same time, one needs to consider that in 1860, there were about seventy times as many whites as free blacks in the United States and that the number of free blacks in many areas where the Underground Railroad was active, like rural Ohio, Indiana and Illinois, was extremely small (and much smaller circa 1850), even though the free blacks who lived in those sections were ready and willing. That also could be said of the Adirondack region, where there were few blacks and almost none with enough material means to provide aid to fugitives from slavery. Although Gara's arguments are cogent and documented, my research in upstate New York revealed a picture that casts some doubt on them.

Union Village was where I had unearthed some serious discoveries when I was doing the Easton study. Siebert had little information about the region. Nearly the only account of consequence was a letter from Troy abolitionist Martin Townsend, who said that the fugitives from slavery were sent through Rouses Point,[18] which borders Canada. Equipped with updated research tools, I was about to change that.

My first find of real substance about the roots of Washington County abolitionism was a report of the organization of the Washington County Anti-Slavery Society in 1834 at Argyle, a hamlet about ten miles north of Union Village. It first appeared in the November 18, 1834 issue of the *Vermont Telegraph* and was reprinted in the *Liberator*, where I found it. Following is a summary.

A convention was held to form an antislavery society in Washington County. It was slated for the Dutch Reformed Church in Argyle. However,

[From the Vermont Telegraph.]

SPIRIT OF THE TIMES—MORE MOBBING.

Fort-Ann, Washington Co. N. Y.
November, 19, 1834.

Brother Murray:

Yesterday the friends of Equal Rights, held a county convention in Washington county, for the purpose of forming a County Anti-Slavery Society. The committee of arrangements had previously obtained permission to occupy the Dutch Reformed church in Argyle, it being in the centre of the county. Accordingly, about 10 or 11 o'clock, the delegates began to assemble. It was soon ascertained, however, that the church had been entered by some ruffians, the doors fastened, and the windows nailed down. An effigy was suspended at the door, representing a Negro, on which was fastened a slip of paper, signed 'Judge Lynch,' containing also four lines of *sublime* poetry, warning abolitionists of their danger from the judge. Some of the members of the convention succeeded in removing the nails, entering a window, and unbarring the door. The meeting soon assembled. The appearance of the delegates indicated decision, nerve, talent and character. The convention was organized by appointing Col. John Straight, President, and Dr. Ira Hatch, and Edwin Andrus, Secretaries. Four committees were appointed—to report resolutions, an address, a constitution, and to nominate officers.

Abolitionists organize the first antislavery society in Washington County.

prior to the meeting, anti-abolitionists had entered the church, nailed the door shut and hung an effigy of a black man at the door with a note of warning signed by "Judge Lynch." Nevertheless, the meeting was held. After a recess, an angry mob gathered at the church and threw out the abolitionists who had remained behind, closing up the church. When the other abolitionists returned, they were threatened with violence, and so the meeting was moved. Some of the mob followed, but they were forced to leave by the landlord of the alternate site. Later, the abolitionists were harassed by a "well dressed fair looking citizen of Argyle," who was an editor of one of the local weekly newspapers.[19]

The report was written by Erastus Culver, a Union Village attorney who would make several widely publicized decisions as a judge in New York City twenty years later that freed fugitives from slavery; his law firm also represented them. Elected president was Dr. Hiram Corliss, also of Union Village, who would be the preeminent abolitionist in the Adirondacks throughout the antebellum period.

Another abolitionist leader in Union Village was Reverend Nathaniel Colver. A rare biography of Colver published in 1873 was provided to me by local historian Sally Brillon. It mentioned an offer that Colver received for a pastorate in Richmond, Virginia, before coming to Union Village and briefly described the trip he made there to consider it.[20] This information enabled me to identify him as the likely writer of an anonymous letter from

Union Village who had been visited by a fugitive from slavery in 1837: "Not 36 hours since, the writer of this note was called on by a colored man who had with him testimonials of the highest character, from several clergymen, and gentlemen known to the to the writer, showing him to have recently been a slave in _____ [space left blank], and now on his way to Canada, a land of freedom."[21]

Considering that I was searching for documented evidence to prove that fugitives from slavery were being aided in Union Village and not relying on secondary accounts, this was an important find. Corroborating this was another discovery: an article that appeared in at least three antislavery publications shortly before the letter to the *Emancipator*, although I didn't find the other two until much later: "A slave of middle age, of noble size, six feet high, had made his escape from the southern States, and passed up the Champlain canal, and from Clinton county, passed through Franklin county, into the north part of St. Lawrence county, with intent to go to Ogdensburgh, and cross over into Canada."[22]

The story was told by central New York abolitionist Alvan Stewart, who learned of the story during an antislavery lecture tour that he made with William L. Chaplin. Stewart provided more details. The fugitive from slavery's destination was Ogdensburg, and he stopped thirty miles from it (about fifteen miles from the St. Lawrence River) to work a few days for a postmaster. While there, a letter from South Carolina addressed to the postmaster in Ogdensburg accidentally fell out on to the ground. It included an advertisement for the fugitive and a reward of $500 for his rendition. The postmaster confronted the fugitive and asked what he should do. The fugitive's reply was that he wished him to do to him as he would if he were the fugitive from slavery. The postmaster replied that the slave was lucky because if the letter had come to the postmaster in Ogdensburg, he surely would have had him apprehended. The postmaster then showed the fugitive slave a more direct route to the river, where he crossed into Canada.[23]

A major factor in the development of the Underground Railroad in Washington County and the Adirondack region in general was the Champlain Canal, which passes through Easton. Completed in 1823, it linked the Hudson River ports of Albany and Troy with Lake Champlain, whose steamboats delivered passengers from the Washington County port of Whitehall to northern New York, Vermont and Canada. The canal was an important commercial thoroughfare for this region during the antebellum period because it made the Adirondacks' rich supply of lumber, iron, coal and grain accessible to the nation's manufacturing centers. Probably making

The Champlain Canal in Washington County.

the greatest use of it was the huge lumber industry that had developed in the region; it had made Albany among the largest lumber traders in the world.[24]

Additional confirmation of regular use of the Champlain Canal by the Underground Railroad during this time was also found in an 1840 letter that I obtained from the Vermont Historical Society. It was written by Troy conductor Reverend Fayette Shipherd to Charles Hicks at Hinesdale in the Vermont town of Bennington: "As the canal has closed I shall send my Southern friends along your road and patronize your house. We had a fine run of business during the season…We had 22 in two weeks, 13 in the city at one time…A Baltimore officer—a man hunter was seen in our city making his observations but left without giving us any trouble. Several slaves were in our city from Baltimore at the time."[25]

In my effort to prove that the Underground Railroad was more than mere legend in Washington County, I found two more primary documents with direct quotes testifying to its activity in Union Village. One was a resolution from an October 8, 1850 meeting condemning the Fugitive Slave Law:

Resolved, In view of the enormities of the present Fugitive Slave Law, its opposition to the spirit of the Constitution framed to establish Justice; and in view of the good character of those in our midst who have escaped from Slavery, that we will obey God who commands su [sic] to hide the outcast and obey the dictates of the Golden Rule—and never, whatever pains and penalties we may suffer, assist into remorseless Slavery those who in our midst may be claimed as Fugitives from the Southern prison-house, but defend to the extent of our duty as Christians, citizens, and men.[26]

A meeting there ten years earlier reported by Reverend Edward C. Pritchett, pastor of the Orthodox Congregational "Free" Church, yielded the following revelation: "While waiting here for the arrival of a fugitive whom we are going to take towards the North Star, I write…"[27] This brief admission shows that aid was being given to a fugitive slave and that information had been passed on ahead about the fugitive's arrival. It demonstrates that a network, an Underground Railroad, was clearly in operation here in 1840.

One of the major tenets of those who are reconsidering the traditional story of the Underground Railroad has been the lack of organization in the Underground Railroad. The spontaneous decisions that often were involved in forwarding fugitives from slavery gave this appearance. However, on the contrary, there was a great deal of organization, and this was the result of the more than 1,350 antislavery societies comprising 120,000 members that had formed in the North by 1838.[28] It was through the network they developed that the tracks of the Underground Railroad were laid down. A microcosm of such organization can be shown in Union Village and later in Easton as well, which worked closely with Union Village in the 1850s, as was implied in the account by Oren B. Wilbur when slave hunters came to the house of the Wilburs.

An insight into how such organization developed can be obtained from an examination of the Orthodox Congregational Free Church in Union Village. It was a "come-outer" church. Its members, under the leadership of Dr. Corliss, left their parent Dutch Reformed Church on account of its refusal to publicly oppose slavery in 1837. The Free Church was not unique or unusual. There were many "come-outer" churches in the North, and all were passionate about abolishing slavery and ready to aid any runaway slave who came to their communities.

Of the local histories, Thurston provided by far the most information about the church, but as I recall, for some reason, I bypassed it because it was

{ UNIONVILLE, WASHINGTON CO.,
} September 1, 1840.

Dear Bro. Goodell,—While waiting here for the arrival of a fugitive whom we are going to take towards the North Star, I write to let you know we have have had a pretty good meeting at Waterford and here, besides other lectures. The Saratoga folks will let you know about their meeting. Here they passed strong resolutions on ecclesiastical and political action, approving the National and State nominations, and called a county meeting for making county nominations, an Monday, Sept. 14, at Argyle, Yours, &c.,
EDWARD C. PRITCHETT.

Above: From Union Village to the North Star.

Left: Dr. Hiram Corliss.

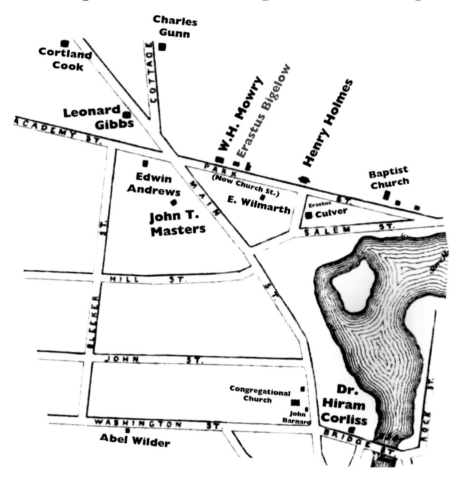

Map showing the residences of Free Church members.

buried in the middle of the book. For the longest time, it seemed, I was aware only of Sharpe's brief reference. However, the cover page of its manual was in the history files of the village library, and my hope was to locate the entire thirty-two-page document. Finally I obtained a copy, I believe, at the state library or possibly through interlibrary loan. It was published in 1860 and contained much information about the church's history, including a list of everyone who had been a member. Using an 1853 map that identified the

The Leonard Gibbs House in Greenwich.

The Mowry House on Park Street in Greenwich.

street numbers and names of the residents, I was able to create a picture of their proximity to one another.

Even more fascinating was the discovery I made by reviewing census records: during the 1850s, blacks were members of the households of leading members of the Free Church. They included the households of John T. Masters, William H. Mowry and Henry Holmes, all trustees of the church, as well as the church founder, Hiram Corliss. What was even more fascinating was another revelation: there was a tunnel that ran under Park Street.

When I gave the presentation at the Easton Library, Greenwich resident Robert Huffman of 1 Cottage Avenue, whose house is almost directly in the path of the houses on Park Street, said that he had found what appears to have been a portion of a tunnel leading from his cellar. Helen Hoag, who lived in Greenwich for more than seventy years, corroborated this and said that she had known about it since she was a child. I can hear the hoots and jeers now from the nabobs of negativity in the halls of ivy. It is a fact, however, that in addition to the account from Oren B. Wilbur, there is a documented account from 1858 of slave hunters attempting the rendition of fugitive from slavery John Salter. His wife, Priscilla Weeks, was listed in the 1850 census as living in the household of Henry Holmes, who lived on Park Street. The account mentions the mobilization of a vigilance committee led by Free Church trustee Leonard Gibbs, who had moved to Union Village in 1845.[29] Gibbs's daughters lived in the village well into the twentieth century and regaled members of the Daughters of the American Revolution with stories about their father's Underground Railroad activities. Thurston's history said that there had been several attempts by slave hunters to reclaim Salter as well.[30]

I never did see or confirm the existence of the tunnel. Hoag's affirmation was good enough for me. She had written an account of Union Village that provided a detailed picture of what it was like in the nineteenth century called *A Walk in the Village*, published in 1997, so if anyone would know about the tunnel, it would be her. Whether or not it was used to protect fugitives from slavery, it is fun to wonder.

No one can deny Union Village's involvement in the Underground Railroad. The evidence is conclusive. That doesn't mean that there isn't more to be discovered. That is the challenge I present to future historians.

Chapter 3

THE STONE CHAIR

Most historians describe the Underground Railroad as loosely organized, noting that conductors usually only knew the next conductor, or at least no more than a few other conductors, along the route. Often this was true. However, as I pointed out in the previous chapter, a network stretching across the country was established during the formation of the antislavery societies in the 1830s. We find story after story about Underground Railroad operatives communicating with other operatives hundreds of miles away or visiting locations hundreds of miles away. Just to name a few, we find agents like Levi Coffin, William Still and Laura Haviland visiting Canada to see fugitives they had helped. We have alumni of Oberlin settling in disparate locations and establishing Underground Railroad stops. We find John Brown knowing the location of the Underground Railroad in far-flung sections. And we see many Underground Railroad conductors traveling hundreds of miles with fugitives from slavery and knowing where to get help, and not just Harriet Tubman.

One of the early works about the Underground Railroad, written by a man who was intimately involved but which serious historians characterize as folklore, was from Fredonia, New York conductor Eber Pettit. His *Sketches in the History of the Underground Railroad*, published in 1879, was a book I read during the early period of my research. His colorful, metaphoric descriptions might seem hyperbolic, but I believe that there is more truth to them than fancy:

The Stone Chair.

No institution has ever existed in this country, whose business was transacted with more perfect fidelity, more profound secrecy, more harmony in the working of its complicated machinery and yet with such tremendous results…It had, like all, other rail roads, its offices and stations, engineers and conductors, ticket agents and train dispatchers, hotels and eating houses…open day and night, and well supplied with the best food the country afforded…The managers availed themselves of all manner of facilities for traveling; rail roads and steam boats, canal boats and ferry boats, stage coaches, gentlemen's carriages and lumber wagons were pressed into active duty when needed.[31]

Union Village and Easton were not the only places where the Underground Railroad operated in the Adirondacks. You couldn't have an Underground Railroad unless there were links between stops. Fugitives from slavery had to come from one place and move on to another. Going north from Union Village, you come to Argyle about ten miles up the road. This was where the county antislavery society formed. The Argyle Presbyterian Church was suspended from its associate synod in 1839 for opposing its position on slavery, and its pastor up until 1851, Reverend James P. Miller, was a passionate abolitionist and staunch member of the Liberty Party and local antislavery societies.[32] Also, church elder Anthony McKallor is alleged to have harbored fugitives from slavery.[33]

An even more fascinating claim is that the house of longtime antebellum village mayor and government official Ransom Stiles was found during an excavation in the 1950s to have a five-hundred-foot tunnel leading from it. This led to speculation at the time that it was used for the Underground Railroad. Another tunnel? Oh my. Why would they have used a tunnel in Argyle, a remote farm town, where it's unlikely that slave hunters would be looking for fugitives from slavery? Yet wasn't Solomon Northup lured into slavery from Saratoga, a mere twenty miles away? Look at what antislavery lecturer Henry C. Wright had to say during a visit to Saratoga in 1853: "Very many slaveholders and slave-hunters are here, some to enjoy the luxuries of our summers, to reconcile the North to slavery and slaveholders, to destroy all conscientious opposition to them, and to hunt fugitives from slavery"[34]

Perhaps the most compelling story about Argyle's role in the Underground Railroad involves Austin and Horace Phillips, twin black boys born at the Argyle Poorhouse sometime during the 1830s (three different dates are reported). It is believed that their parents were fugitives from slavery who left them behind. Eventually, the boys were taken in by local families. "Oss," who served in the Civil War, lived most of his life in Washington County and died in 1918 in Glens Falls, never knew who his parents were or what became of them.[35] What is puzzling about the Argyle Poorhouse is that official records show no admittance of black persons from 1835 to 1859, which is incredulous, although one date for the Phillips twins' birth was given as 1833.[36] This suggests that it may have been regularly used to harbor fugitives from slavery like the Phillips parents were.

Moving north and crossing the Champlain Canal, we come to Fort Edward and the old Fort Museum, a residence for a time of Solomon Northup. Farther north through Hudson Falls in the town of Kingsbury, we come to more farm country, where one of the more bizarre artifacts of the Underground Railroad sits alongside Vaughn Road. Made of stone and about the size of a tombstone, it's shaped like a chair. It once had legs, but they were destroyed by a roadwork crew in the 1930s that was unaware of its possible significance, said Kingsbury town historian Paul Loding when I interviewed him in 1999.[37]

What makes the stone even more intriguing is that in addition to the date chiseled on it—May 23, 1841—there are hieroglyphics, faded over time, that appear to be representations of actual things or places. A drawing made in the 1930s in the possession of Loding is more discernible.

Local historians have puzzled over the purpose of this strange artifact, and the best they have come up with is that it served as a map for fugitives from slavery heading north. According to Loding, the hieroglyphics show a triangular shape on the left and what looks like a smokestack behind it. On the right is what looks like a flag atop a building and, behind that, a sailboat. If you look at the chair, you would be looking north, and in that direction on the left is Putnam Mountain and, behind it, what was the Mount Hope Blast Furnace, which explains the smokestack; the triangular shape with the flag above on the middle-right represents Fort Ann and, behind that, the inlet to Lake Champlain, the ultimate destination for fugitives from slavery and a place where they could get a boat to Canada.

Who created the stone chair? Most have believed that it was black preacher Reverend George S. Brown, a native of Rhode Island who came to the area in 1827, the year slavery was outlawed in New York. At the time, he was a wandering minstrel outfitted with bagpipes, oboe, clarinet and other instruments. Religion was not part of his life, and he stopped to take work at a farm in Kingsbury. He ended up staying and was converted to Christianity. Tradition claims that he was an excellent stonemason, and to this day, there are houses and stone walls alleged to be the result of his handiwork.

The Guideboard sign.

Another interesting remnant of the Underground Railroad less than a half a mile from the Stone Chair on Vaughn Corners Road is an extraordinary sign that locals call the old "Underground Railway Guideboard." It depicts a caricature of a black man in a black tuxedo and top hat, carrying a cane. He's pointing north, "4½ miles to Fort Ann." This sign is of fairly recent vintage.

Why would such a sign exist in this rural section, where there are no blacks for miles? Locals say that it was painted by a man named Collins Doubleday, whose family owned the land on which it sits at least as early as 1853, according to period maps. Furthermore, the current sign is not the original. Sometime around 1930, the sign replaced another that showed only a hand pointing north, according to Fort Ann town historian Virginia Parrott, whom I interviewed in 1999. Sterling Harrington, whose ancestors bought the house from the Doubledays, said that the sign originally was placed on an elm tree in the middle of the intersection of Vaughn and Bentley Roads. There also were two other signs on the tree, one that directed travelers to Smith's Basin, through which the Champlain Canal passes. Charles Willis, another local who grew up in Kingsbury, said that old-timers claimed that they'd hide the fugitives from slavery in the area's root cellars, of which there were several. Delilah Chesterman, who grew up in the Doubleday house, offered another intriguing piece of folklore. She said that she used to ride her horse as a girl along a nearby trail that led directly to Fort Ann that was called by locals the "Underground Railroad." She had no idea where the name came from. This leads us to Fort Ann, through which the Champlain Canal passes, as well as the location of the Goodman Farm and the Old Stone Library, two more legendary stops, only ten miles south of Lake Champlain.

In about 1998, I was able to arrange a meeting (thanks to Sally Brillon) with the Washington County Historical Society president, John Mead. He agreed to sponsor me for a grant that would lead to the eventual publication by the society of my book about the Underground Railroad in Washington County. There was no contract, just a verbal agreement. This sponsorship continued for two years, such that I was able to obtain two other small grants from the funding institution. Consequently, I was invited to be the guest speaker during that period for the annual dinner meeting of the society. I usually try to do something different when it's a special occasion, and with the help of my friend Shirley McFerson, we came up with a creative idea.

As I said, Shirley was a colorful lady who liked to perform. I don't recall who came up with the scenario. I made some introductory remarks and then introduced the special guest, the fortuneteller "Madame Yemaya." She told the audience that she was going to conduct a séance and attempt to recall the voices of some of the departed abolitionists from Washington County and the vicinity. She stressed that everyone needed to concentrate on the persons whose names I had given to her to try to recall.

While Madame Yemaya regaled the audience, I went into a back room and turned on the microphone that we had connected to speakers in the banquet room and prepared to read the scripts that, in part, quoted from words these abolitionists had used in letters, diaries or other documents. The first of the six voices was the man who was at the head of all the abolitionists in the county from the day he became involved, the county's unequivocal leader, Dr. Hiram Corliss, and last to be heard was Esther Wilbur. The abolitionist with the most poignant words was the eminent judge Erastus T. Culver: "Those were times of great sorrow and rejoicing for the oppressed people we assisted," his "spirit" recalled. "A time to weep at the loss of home and loved ones, but also a time to rejoice at the birth of their liberty. Wherever there be those oppressed, they must be let free."

As a postscript to this chapter, I finished a forty-two-thousand-word manuscript on the Underground Railroad in Washington County and submitted it to the historical society during the summer of 2000. I also had discovered two more especially rich accounts of antislavery meetings in the county. One occurred in 1851, when British abolitionist and orator George Thompson headlined the meeting. Other speakers were Abby Kelley Foster and Sojourner Truth, who was as yet little known.[38] The second account was the organizational meeting of the Old Saratoga Anti-Slavery Society, which was a merger of residents from Union Village, Easton and Quaker Springs, a community across the Hudson River from Easton. Elected president was, as expected, Hiram Corliss. Elected as one of the three vice-presidents was John Wilbur. Samuel Wilbur was elected as secretary and Job Wilbur, Esther's husband, as treasurer. There were other Wilburs mentioned as well. The special guests were William Lloyd Garrison and Parker Pillsbury. Corliss remarked on the society's steadfast adherence to "higher law" principles, and the meeting made several resolutions opposing the work of the Colonization Society.[39]

When John Mead's term as president of the historical society ended, a meeting was scheduled to discuss the publication of my manuscript. Unfortunately, the change of administration caused a problem. Because we didn't have a written contract with the terms of our agreement, the new team had different ideas than John, who had already moved out of the area. They said that they would publish the book but with the stipulation that all royalties go to the society. They reasoned that because I had received money from the grants to work on the book, which they sponsored, all the proceeds for the sale should go to them. I refused. Now I had to look for a new publisher, which allowed me to expand my horizons and my research.

Chapter 4
THE FORGOTTEN ABOLITIONIST

Short, slight and looking younger than his years, Reverend Charles T. Torrey did not look the part of someone who would defy brutal slave hunters in that year of our Lord, 1841. But Charles was a man with a fiery resolve to end slavery. Nothing else mattered. He had quit his pastorate to devote himself to the cause, leaving behind his wife and two young daughters to assault the monstrous institution in Washington, D.C. Yes, in this nation whose creed claimed that "All Men Are Created Equal," slave pens were plentiful, and slave trading took place within sight of the nation's capitol. He was fearless but a bit naïve. It's not a good idea to go into the South and tell everyone that you're an abolitionist. Earlier that year, he had been arrested and spent time in jail because his presence had not been welcomed at a slaveholders' convention, which he was attending as a journalist. As he was writing a letter to his wife, there was a knock at his door. He rose from his desk.

"Who calls there?"

"It's Thomas." Thomas Smallwood was a former slave who had been freed eleven years earlier and was full of righteous indignation about his former status. He had introduced himself to Torrey after his release from jail, and they had formed a partnership to establish a track of the Underground Railroad, a daring enterprise even in the North but a life-threatening undertaking in the South.

Torrey opened the door to his apartment in the boardinghouse. Smallwood was a larger, older man, and yet it was the younger man, Torrey, who was in command.

"So, is everything ready?"

"Yes, I have brought the horses and wagon," Smallwood said. "Everyone is at the church."

Torrey retrieved his belongings and closed up his apartment. He had paid up his landlady and told her that he would probably be leaving that evening. They went outside into the

ABOLITIONISM.—We take the following from the Tocsin of Liberty, the organ of the Abolitionists, published at Albany.

"*Twenty six Slaves in one week.*—Sam. Weller is requested to tell the slave-holders that we passed twenty-six prime slaves to the land of freedom last week, and several more this week thus far. Don't know what the end of the week will foot up. All went by ' the underground railroad.'

" Tell Mary Wrightson, Cook's Point, Maryland, that Moses Giles wishes to be remembered to her as an old acquaintance, and that he was well and in good spirits, and liked liberty very much.

" Henry Hawkins would like to have Sam inform Austin Scott, at Washington City, that he is well, and is delighted with Northern scenery and society, and hopes he may get along without his services in future. He wants him to send the editor of the Tocsin money enough to buy a new coat, as the linen roundabout is nearly worn out, and it is coming on cold soon. This would only be a *very* small item in the amount of which Scott has robbed him of his services."

Now these abolition committee-men could just as honestly aid in smuggling away thirty-six stolen horses, or bales of stolen goods, as to aid in the nefarious business of which they boast to their shame.

Sam Weller was the pen name of Thomas Smallwood.

dusky evening. The large Conestoga wagon had a nice cover to conceal his passengers. Torrey patted the heads of his lead horses. Smallwood sat next to him as they set out, but he was only going along for the ride to retrieve the freedom seekers. He would stay behind and continue his efforts running the Underground Railroad, while Torrey would remain in New York and look for work to support his family.

After retrieving the fifteen freedom seekers, who included women and children, and saying goodbye to Smallwood, Torrey set out on the road to Rockville, Maryland, with his flock. At the time, most took the turnpike to Baltimore to head north, which was a more direct route. Torrey thought it better to go west and then cut back east toward Baltimore on another road that they could pick up in Rockville, decreasing their chances of being confronted by a slave patrol. In the past, they would hire teamsters for the job. This time, circumstances required Torrey to lead them. Advertisements had been published for the fugitives from slavery, in some cases multiple notices, but it had been a while since their escapes. The time seemed right to take that final step to freedom as their trail had grown cold.

The ride was smooth sailing at first, and the summer stars kept Torrey awake while his passengers mostly slept. Smallwood had supplied them with plenty of water and other provisions, and Torrey only stopped when necessary for the comfort of his passengers. As the night approached dawn, however, a problem with one of the wheels had developed, and he was forced to pull off into the bushes. He and some of the men were looking to see if they could fix it when they heard the sound of hoof beats. They became silent. Covered by the thick underbrush in the dim light of dawn, they were well concealed, though they could see out from their position. It was five men on horseback, and they looked like a slave patrol. Their wagon problem turned out to be a lucky break. Fortunately, they were near their first stop along the Underground Railroad and were able to arrive before the wheel gave out. Their host found them a new wagon while they rested during the daylight.

When night fell again, they resumed their journey. Their biggest challenge was to cross the Susquehanna River, about forty miles distant. They would not chance taking the quicker route by using the ferry at Havre de Grace, Maryland, for it was almost certain that it would arouse suspicion and lead to their capture before crossing the Mason-Dixon line. The plan was to use the ferry at Peach Bottom, just a few miles over the Mason-Dixon line in Pennsylvania. Just a few miles away, there was the good Quaker Joseph Smith of Drumore, who was always ready to help weary freedom seekers.

This time, their wagon held up. It was early morning when they reached the ferry, and the boat was available to take them across. Within a short time, they reached the farm of Friend Smith and another day of rest and refreshment before resuming their journey north to New York. Now in a section populated with many Quakers and free black citizens who were active in the Underground Railroad, it felt like they were on the brink of the Promised Land.

Several days later, Torrey was home with his family and writing to Smallwood that he had made a successful journey and had forwarded his passengers on the Champlain Canal to Canada and a new life of freedom. He was about to enter into another partnership with a like-minded abolitionist who was every bit afire as Torrey to free the slaves: Reverend Abel Brown.[10]

We fast-forward some 150 years later. While my expectations to have my book published encountered a roadblock, I was expanding my research and coming up with new discoveries. I had come across an entry in the catalogue at the state library that drew my interest. It listed an abolitionist newspaper,

PROSPECTUS OF THE LIFE AND WRITINGS OF REV. ABEL BROWN.

C. S. Brown proposes to publish the life of her late husband, Rev. Abel Brown, including many of his private journals and letters, together with an account of his labors in various causes of reform, particularly in connection with the temperance and anti-slavery movements of the age. The opposition and persecution he encountered in the form of mobs, indictments, &c., will be given ; also an account of his travels, in connection with his wife and partner in the anti-slavery enterprise. The work will comprise from 250 to 300 pages, good sized duodecimo, and will be illustrated by wood engravings. Price 50 cents, bound in muslin : twelve copies for five dollars.

The authorised Agents to receive subscriptions are as follows : Albany, William L. Chaplin, T. Townsend and Julius R. Ames ; Troy, Rev. H. H. Garnet, Rev. Fayette Shipherd ; Poughkeepsie, Rev. C. Van Loon ; Utica, Alvan Stewart ; Canandaigua, J. Mosher.

A request for material for a book on Reverend Abel Brown.

the *Albany Patriot*. I had never heard of it. The rare book and manuscript department said that it was in a warehouse where they stored items that were seldom requested, but they weren't sure and needed to do a search. I put it out of my mind. After about a month, I got a call that they had found it—a run of two years of issues. It sounded fascinating.

When I first saw the yellowing tabloid attached to a big green binder, I couldn't wait to take a look. The oversized pages were rather heavy compared to a modern newspaper, and they gave me gloves to turn the pages. I found articles about many of the abolitionists in the Adirondacks, some written by men like Hiram Corliss and Reverend James Miller. I found that they belonged to the Eastern New York Anti-Slavery Society, whose membership was connected by their residence in counties through which the Hudson River passed.[11]

I also found another entry that first day that piqued my curiosity. A widow was requesting material for her book about her late husband, Reverend Abel

Brown, to be included with "many of his private journals and letters, together with an account of his labors in various causes of reform, particularly in connection with the temperance and anti-slavery movements of the age." I wondered who he was and whether she ever wrote the book.

I decided to try the SUNY-Albany library. To my surprise, I found it in the card catalogue. When I reached its location in the stacks, I found this little golden book exactly where it was supposed to be. I couldn't believe it. Here it was, printed in 1849 and available for circulation. What luck, or maybe it was fate. Sometimes I think an unseen power led me to Reverend Abel Brown, a man who had been forgotten, who in his time was both hated and beloved—hated because he passionately espoused an unpopular cause and beloved because of the totally selfless personal aid and comfort he provided those who were so desperately in need.

The book was a veritable gold mine, filled with stories about Brown's efforts in the antislavery cause, and it included a number of anecdotes about his aid to fugitives from slavery, as well as their personal stories. It also detailed a number of lecture tours he took into the far reaches of the Adirondacks, visiting with abolitionists like Joseph Leggett in Chestertown and Noadiah Moore in Champlain, Clinton County, New York, near the Canadian border. On many of his tours, he was accompanied by black lecturers like Lewis Washington and James Baker, fugitives from slavery who became active in the abolition movement. Brown, I also learned, was the organizer of the aforementioned Eastern New York Anti-Slavery Society, whose president was none other than Hiram Corliss. I wondered what authorities on abolitionism might know about him. I contacted a member of the then newly formed New York State Freedom Trail Commission, Syracuse University history professor Milton Sernett, who was an acknowledged expert. No, Milt said, he had never heard of him. But the biography claimed that Brown aided more than one thousand fugitives from slavery.

I had to get the Abel Brown story out, and I found a monthly in the Catskill region, *Homestyle* magazine, that focused on the arts. I submitted a piece entitled "Abel Brown: Forgotten Abolitionist," which noted in part:

> *The Underground Railroad holds secrets that never will be uncovered. Too much time has passed. Most of the stations no longer exist, many of the records have been destroyed, the still hidden tunnels are eroding, and the people have turned to dust. Yet their spirits live on. Rev. Abel Brown, a forgotten abolitionist who died at 34 in 1844, is among those whose deeds echo through history.*

The Tocsin of Liberty,

Published Weekly, at Albany, N. Y.

BY ELDER ABEL BROWN,

Under the special patronage of the

ALBANY LIBERTY ASSOCIATION.

**At $1.50 per annum to Companies of 10,
Or $2.00 the single copy, per mail,**

ALWAYS IN ADVANCE.

Devoted to Freedom—Equality—Temperance—Virtue
—Agriculture—Commerce—Legislative Proceedings —
The News of the Day, Foreign and Domestic—The Arts
and Sciences—Trades—Select Miscellany, &c.

OFFICE No. 56 (UP STAIRS,) STATE-STREET.

☞ Ministers of the Gospel, Lecturing Agents, and
others, are requested to act as Agents.

Clergymen who obtain for us two subscribers and send
us FOUR DOLLARS in advance, free of postage, or SIX DOL-
LARS and Four subscribers, will receive our paper a
year gratis.

. A liberal commission to travelling agents. Ad-
dress the publisher, Albany, N. Y.   Jan. 4, 1842.

Those editors who will insert the above, shall have
a like favor from us.

Masthead of the *Tocsin of Liberty*.

*Born in Springfield, MA, he began his ministry at age 22, preaching the
cause of Temperance. He would not compromise under any circumstance
and this made his life a series of confrontations.*[42]

Abel Brown was much like Charles Torrey, and I actually discovered him
before I learned of Torrey, who was for a time his collaborator in publishing
the *Albany Patriot* and its earlier incarnation, the *Tocsin of Liberty*.

Both worked together in establishing the Underground Railroad between
Washington, D.C., and Albany. One of their boldest and most innovative

SOUTHERN MEANNESS.—The following letter and advertisement were received by mail, with a charge of 56 cents postage, a few days since :

$100 REWARD.—Run away from the subscriber, in Baltimore city, on Thursday, 25th ult. a *Mulatto Man*, named *Robert Hill*. [We omit the description.]

WALTER FERNANDIS.

The letter was addressed inside to " The Abolitionist BROWN."

REPLY.

MR. FERNANDIS—This is to inform you that the noble Robert Hill reached this city in safety, and was safely sent on his way rejoicing. We charge you $25 for money paid him and services rendered, and 56 cents for the letter containing the advertisement. Please send a draft for the same. ABEL BROWN,
Forwarding Merchant, Albany.

P. S.—The business is very good this year. Please inform the slaves that we are always on hand ready to receive them. A. B.

From the *Vermont Freeman*, July 1, 1843.

techniques was to publish ads in the *Tocsin* announcing their aid to fugitives from slavery and taunting their masters, a kind of counterpoint to the typical "wanted" fugitive slave ads that were ubiquitous in southern newspapers during the antebellum period.

Brown, like Torrey, had gone into the South to bring out slaves when he had lived in Beaver, Pennsylvania, a town along the Ohio River near Pittsburgh.[13] If ever there were twin souls, it would be Brown and Torrey, and both, sadly, were to die before they reached their thirty-fifth birthdays—

Brown succumbing to a breakdown from exhaustion in Canandaigua, New York, while on an antislavery lecture tour and Torrey in 1846 while in a Maryland prison for aiding fugitives from slavery. They were martyrs to the cause, like Elijah Lovejoy and John Brown.

The article created some interest, and Stephen Zielinski of the New York State Museum, who was organizing the 1999 Conference on New York State History the following summer, arranged for me to be part of the panel discussion on the Underground Railroad to introduce my information about Brown. The forgotten abolitionist was no longer to be forgotten.

I still remember how nervous I was speaking before an academic audience. I was trying to make a splash, but I have never have been the most facile public speaker. The introduction of an unknown person who played an important role in New York State history, however, compensated. At the conference, held in Oneonta, I met two important historians of abolitionism whose books and studies have aided me in my efforts over the years: Judy Wellman, now professor emeritus at SUNY-Oswego, and Graham Hodges, professor of history at Colgate University. It was my introduction to serious students of history. I still have a ways to go to measure up.

As for Abel Brown, he died in Canandaigua. Funeral services were held there and in Troy, the latter being performed by the noted black abolitionist Henry Highland Garnet.[44] The *American Freeman*, an abolitionist paper in Prairieville, Wisconsin Territory, where Brown lectured on his western tour in 1843, published a lengthy obituary, an excerpt of which follows:

> *He sustained for the last four years past, the relation of Agent to the Eastern N.Y. Anti-Slavery Society. In every department of the Anti-Slavery enterprise, he exhibited a spirit that could not rest while so much was at stake and so much required to be done. In circulating anti-slavery publications, in urging religious denominations to practice the principles they avowed, and…in assisting, as a member of the vigilance committee, trembling Americans, to the number of not less than one thousand…He was a pattern to believers—a living argument against unbelief.*[45]

Chapter 5

198 LUMBER STREET

For most people, what's past is past; it's what happens today and tomorrow that matters. But nothing is truer than the cliché that those who neglect the past will be condemned to repeat it. We see this happen time and again with important decisions made by government or rules fashioned in any number of societies. We also see it in our own lives as we repeat some of the mistakes we thought we'd never make again. It's human nature to neglect the past. It's what life is all about—living in the moment, living for today.

Historians, however, at the very least, understand the value of the past and try to make it available so that we don't keeping making the same mistakes. This was part of my task, my goal as a seeker of the historical truth, and as I was expanding my research efforts, I reached out to one of the nation's historic treasure-troves, the foremost keeper of early American history, the American Antiquarian Society (AAS) in Worcester, Massachusetts.

It's an impressive, domed, brick structure with a Greco-Roman pediment and columns at the entrance and Federal-style ornamentation. The library itself celebrated its 200th anniversary in 2012. The current building was completed in 1924, and it has had a number of additions since to house its more than 4 million items related to American history, literature and visual culture, making it the largest collection of printed materials through 1876 in North America and the West Indies.

I knew little about it when I took my first journey there, only that it was a great place to do research. Worcester is a good two-hour-plus ride from my home, which was then in Schenectady, New York. It was only one of the many road trips I have made along my journey into the past and my search for the withheld history of the Underground Railroad. I had done some searching in AAS's online catalogue before arriving and had printed a long list of materials I wanted to see, a list far too long to complete in one day.

In any case, I arrived early that morning and went to work. Among the myriad materials I requested was a broadside. The term was new to me. Simply put, they were advertisements printed on posters. This particular broadside was listed as follows: "*Vigilance Committee Office.* Broadside. Albany, N.Y., July 1856." It was the name "Vigilance Committee" that jumped out for me—this was a euphemism often used to describe a group involved in the Underground Railroad.

When it was presented to me, I was surprised to see how big it was. I have a framed copy of it today, and it measures eleven by seventeen inches, though I believe the original is actually bigger. Now, you must be wondering why I framed a broadside printed in 1856. Well, for one reason, it stated that the vigilance committee had aided 287 fugitives from slavery in the prior nine months. Guess that's pretty good evidence that there was an Underground Railroad operating in Albany. It also reported the committee's expenses for boarding and transporting the fugitives from slavery and asked for contributions to help them continue in their good work. The address of the office was listed as 198 Lumber Street. Even better, it listed the names of the vigilance committee, as well as its general agent and superintendent, Stephen Myers.

Fascinating, but I wasn't sure what to make of it. I didn't know much about Stephen Myers, although I recalled mention of him by Frederick Douglass in his autobiography as Albany's Underground Railroad "superintendent."[46] I had the broadside copied and later made my own copies and distributed some at an organizational meeting of the New York State Society for the Preservation of the Underground Railroad, which was being formed by a young man, Patrick Sorsby, with aggressive support from his mother.

I believe Sorsby got the idea for his organization after seeing a few of my columns about the Underground Railroad in the *Chronicle*, the Glens Falls weekly for which I wrote music reviews and arts features. He seemed very enthusiastic at first and persuaded me to volunteer some press releases for him. I also was one of the featured speakers at his organizational meeting. His goal was to develop a museum devoted to the Underground Railroad in Hudson Falls. The meeting was held at the Hyde Collection, the Glens Falls art museum and chamber music venue, and had a reasonable turnout.

I didn't hear back from Sorsby. I learned that he had created an exhibit in the storefront window of a business in downtown Glens Falls. I don't

Paul and Mary Liz Stewart, founders of the Underground Railroad History Project of the Capital District in Albany, New York. *Courtesy Paul and Mary Liz Stewart.*

even recall now what was exhibited. It was the last public effort that he made, as I heard he was turning his attention to law school. In any case, our brief association intersected with what was then another neophyte Underground Railroad organization in Albany, which brings us full circle to Stephen Myers.

Paul and Mary Liz Stewart are from Albany, New York, and have a passionate interest in the Underground Railroad. Mary is a retired grade school teacher, and Paul works for a bank. They were fairly well informed about Stephen Myers, as much as they could be, because although Myers is in some of the Albany history books, there isn't much about him. One of our first meetings was on a Saturday afternoon to track down the Albany locations of the Underground Railroad. I had identified many of the city's abolitionists through reports of antislavery meetings that I had collected, and I had searched through the city directories for their addresses. These were available at the main branch of the Albany Public Library.

The Stewarts were preparing a walking tour and planning to base the tour around what we found. But we weren't very successful: we turned up only two other houses in addition to the vigilance committee office on Livingston

Avenue, the modern name of Lumber Street. One was the residence of an abolitionist active in antislavery societies, and the other was the residence of one of those named on the vigilance committee broadside. Many of the locations were parking lots or places of business. I didn't hear back from them and wondered what happened. I learned through a third party that they were told that the vigilance committee broadside I found at the Antiquarian Society had other claimants. Patrick Sorsby had told them that he found the copy I gave him in an attic in Hudson Falls. Apparently, the Stewarts called the AAS, and for some reason, it was unable to locate it, temporarily. Finally, the staff found it, and I was given a reprieve.

The Stewarts and I mended fences, and I became a regular participant at their annual Underground Railroad conference until I moved from New York in 2005, although I did go back for one in 2009. They took that broadside and ran with it. They discovered that the house that was at the address indicated by the broadside was not the actual site of the vigilance committee office, which was also the home of Stephen Myers. It was the building next door; it turned out that the numbers on the street had changed. It was a good thing because the original house we had thought was the site was about ready to be condemned. The correct house, however, is a fine urban brownstone. They have raised large sums of money to renovate and preserve it for posterity, and in the near future, it will become a museum.

I'm happy to have played a role in their enterprise. That's the role of a researcher like me—to pass on the information to those who can use it for the good of society. It's fitting that all three of us were winners in 2008 of the first annual Underground Railroad Free Press awards, me for the advancement of knowledge and the Stewarts for historic preservation.

Regarding the importance of Myers, Paul had found a substantial article about him in Peter Ripley's *The Black Abolitionist Papers*, an important and huge five-volume work on black antebellum history. He also turned me on to Myers's abolitionist newspaper, the *Northern Star and Freeman's Advocate*, of which a number of issues from 1842 to 1843 are available on microfilm at the SUNY-Albany library. There were only two references to aiding fugitives from slavery in the issues I saw, however. The broadside was the key, and it turned out that it was not the only one Myers published.

Another, called "Circular to the Friends of Freedom," was published on March 29, 1858, announcing aid to 121 fugitives from slavery during the previous six months. The copy of the broadside that I obtained, also at the AAS, included a letter on the back to Francis Jackson of the Boston Vigilance Committee, dated May 22, 1858. It reported aiding 67 fugitives from slavery

The Stephen and Harriet Myers House in Albany.

during the previous six weeks. Myers obviously was a busy man. In fact, his main source of income was coming from his work with fugitives from slavery, as he confessed in this second broadside: "We devote all our time to the care of the oppressed. Our pay is small, but yet we are willing to continue to do what we can for them."

In a second section of the broadside, Myers made another appeal for subscriptions, saying that "we have not received enough to meet the necessary expenses of the Underground Railroad." However, Myers also received funds from editors Thurlow Weed of the *Albany Evening Journal* and Horace Greeley of the *New York Tribune*; New York governors William H. Seward, John Alsop King and Edward D. Morgan; New York City merchants

Moses Grinnell, Simeon Draper and Robert B. Minturn; philanthropist James W. Beekman; Livingston County, New York patrician General James Wadsworth, considered to be the richest man in the Union army and who died in the Civil War; New York City contractor John P. Cummings; Albany stone manufacturer William Newton; and John Jay of Westchester County, the grandson of the Founding Father.[17] Quite an elite and wealthy list. Stephen certainly wasn't starving, although he was a hard worker and had been a boatman since the 1830s. In the *Northern Star*, he reported that fugitives from slavery had been coming to Albany on boats since 1831.[18]

I also found more references to Myers in newspapers during the 1850s (and he is noted in Sidney Howard Gay's "Record of Fugitives 1855–"), during which fifty-four fugitives from slavery were sent to Albany. The one to me that is an eye-opener, however, and that provides an explanation for how so many fugitives from slavery were coming through his office, was an article in the May 10, 1848 issue of the *Albany Patriot* that described the *Armenia*, a steamer that made daily trips between New York City and Albany; coincidentally, Myers worked on this ship.

It was a "neat, swift, little day-boat from New York to Troy" that could make the trip from New York to Albany in nine hours, and "nothing on the river is likely to slip by her in any fair contest." The boat's design was marked by a novel "improvement…the table is set on the first deck instead of below, as is usual…A light, airy saloon, of a hot or a dark day, is altogether more comfortable than a close and dungeon-like place." Its steward was Myers, whose surname was given and of whom it said, "He really does up the thing, with the support of his assistants, in just about the best style. Stephen has had a long experience in the culinary department, and can't be beat by white folks."[49]

On the surface, this description might mean nothing to the average reader, but when you consider the context, it begins to take on more meaning. For instance, it claims that the *Armenia* was the fastest boat on the river, which is an important factor if you need to outrace a slave catcher trying to retrieve his fugitives from slavery. Also, the dining tables are atop the deck instead of below. Does that suggest that perhaps fugitives from slavery are being hidden below? Finally, we come to the ship's steward, Stephen Myers, one of the Underground Railroad's most prolific conductors. Even more compelling is that this ship made daily runs to New York City, where my research puts a conservative estimate of five thousand fugitives from slavery having being aided from 1835 to 1860 (see the appendix). This is based on numerous newspaper and vigilance committee reports that were published during that period. Stephen may have been devoting more time to cooking when

Model of the *Armenia* at the Mariner's Museum, Newport News, Virginia.

working on the *Armenia*, but that doesn't explain why a radical abolitionist newspaper known for its involvement in the Underground Railroad would print an article about a pleasure boat.

One thing I learned during this experience is that history can be a territorial thing. For example, one local historian I met had said that she had been researching the Underground Railroad for thirty to forty years. She had found some incredible stories but said that she couldn't reveal them because she was going to use them for a book someday—a book still unwritten seventeen years later. Another time, I was asked to withhold information by a colleague for a project we were working on. I spilled the beans to another historian, whom I asked to keep it confidential. The next thing I knew, everyone knew about it. What can you do? No one owns history. It has already happened. The best thing we can do is share it with everyone we know. That's the only way it can have value. That's why we are historians.

In any case, what matters is that Stephen Myers's life was a tireless effort to further the rights of African Americans and to defend the freedom of fugitives from slavery. The following appeal, written by him in the January 2, 1843 issue of the *Northern Star*, sums up the mission of his life: "[L]et the voice of forty thousand colored citizens be heard at the Capitol of the Empire state; yes, and at Washington, until the prayers of two millions and a half be heard that are now held in abject bondage, and that Congress may not turn their petitions away unheard as formerly; and let us see American slavery immediately abolished from our land."

Chapter 6
THEY PULLED ALL THE ROPES

All aboard! This train's bound for the Promised Land. Where fugitives from slavery sought freedom in those explosive days before the Civil War. When the slavery question was the talk of the country. And when the words "Underground Railroad" were spoken in hushed tones.

Those were the opening words of my first column about the Underground Railroad that I wrote for the *Chronicle*, the Glens Falls weekly. Editor and publisher Mark Frost agreed to periodically publish a series of columns on various topics related to the local Underground Railroad. About a dozen were published over a period of a few years. It gave me good exposure and led to numerous invitations to speak locally. This covered the period from late 1998 through the year 2000, when the opportunity to publish a book had come and gone and also during the time when I discovered Abel Brown's biography and the Stephen Myers broadside. I didn't mention either of those discoveries in the column because they dealt with Albany and were not in the *Chronicle*'s coverage area.

After my disappointing experience with the Washington County Historical Society, I looked for new support. A new historical society had formed in Warren County, so I contacted it and was put in touch with its then acting president, Marilyn Van Dyke. She was a recently retired grade school principal and the Queensbury Town historian. I told her about my research, and she expressed interest in working together on a project to study the Underground Railroad in Warren County. We set up a meeting.

You never know what to expect when you meet someone, but we clicked from the start. Before long, a project to map out and tell the story of the Underground Railroad in Warren County was developed. Marilyn is a forward-looking lady, and she became enthused when I suggested that we do a PowerPoint presentation with audio. She expanded on the idea to put it on CD-ROM and make it available to local schools. She also wanted to create a brochure with a map and information about Warren County locations that were possible stops. Even better, Marilyn said that she would coordinate the submission of grants to cover some of the cost of my time. This kind of reception to my work more than made up for my bad experience with Washington County.

It was about eight years then since I had written that first article for the *Post-Star*, the Glens Falls daily. I had known almost nothing about the Underground Railroad. I had spent most of my time since then studying Washington County, and now I had a chance to revisit the stories from which I originally learned about the Underground Railroad and give them more intelligent scrutiny.

One of my first tasks was to map out the locations of the Boyd and Stoddard families. I was able to do that using an antebellum map that showed the names of city residents at their locations and found that they lived on the same block, only a short distance from the Hudson River, along which Glens Falls sits. One of the local histories claimed that there was a Quaker family on Jay Street only a few blocks away. This street dead-ends at the river. I also found that two other individuals who were known abolitionists, Cyrus Burnham and George Hawley, were neighbors, only two blocks from the Boyd and Stoddard families.

As Boyd noted in his 1927 account, "The village became a station on the so-called underground railroad, which aided any fugitive slave to reach the Canadian border and freedom. Many of our prominent citizens knew all the ropes and helped pull them."[50]

The area that drew my greatest attention was Chestertown. I had found a passage in the Abel Brown biography that talked of dining with Joseph Leggett and his wife, as well as staying at the Temperance Tavern,[51] now the home of Jane Parrott, who was the first person I interviewed about the Underground Railroad. Leggett also was mentioned in a report from Gerrit Smith of his antislavery lecture tour in the Adirondacks that was published in the *Albany Patriot*, the newspaper that was in that big green binder I tracked down at the state library.[52] In addition, I found briefs reporting Liberty Party meetings in Chestertown as late as 1851 and noting that Joseph Leggett was president of the local chapter.

That they were Liberty Party members is significant. This group formed in 1840 following a split in the antislavery movement between the followers

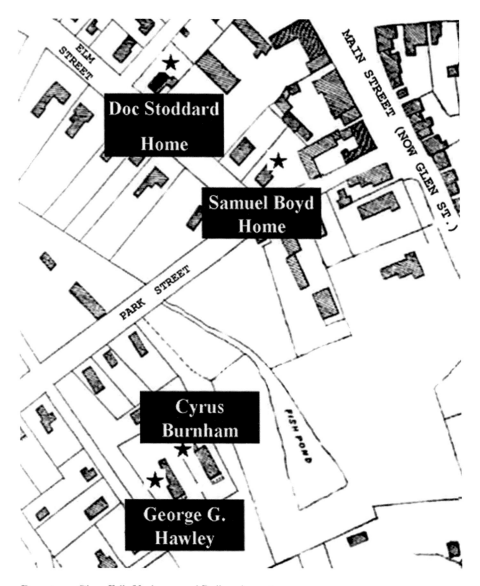

Downtown Glens Falls Underground Railroad agents.

of William Lloyd Garrison, who believed in using only moral suasion (ethical arguments) to end slavery, and those who felt that this was insufficient and that political action was necessary. Most of those in the Liberty Party were more devoutly religious than the Garrisonians, especially considering that

The Temperance Tavern in nineteenth-century Chestertown. *Courtesy Town of Chester historian.*

many of the Garrisonians were at odds with the nation's churches because their hierarchies refused to condemn slavery. Many of the Liberty Party advocates, however, formed their own "come-outer" churches, as in Union Village, where Hiram Corliss and all the abolitionists were Liberty Party members, except for Erastus Culver, who was a Whig. Other Liberty Party members, like Abel Brown and Charles Torrey, both of whom were ministers, condemned their parent churches and made their religion a war on slavery. In many cases, Liberty Party members were more fervent in their antislavery, and in later years, its former members made up the radical fringe that advocated violence to overthrow slavery, such as John Brown and Frederick Douglass. Because most of the abolitionists in the Adirondacks were Liberty Party members, who believed in the higher law and that "obedience to slavery was disobedience to God," it's understandable that they would have no qualms about breaking the law and aiding fugitives from slavery.

With an eye on visiting the Leggett House, which was unoccupied, I contacted one of the family members, Craig Leggett, who lived in Vermont. He gladly agreed to meet me at the house and discuss his family's history, as well as to see if we could find some remnant that might be linked to the

Left: Joseph Leggett. *Courtesy Dan Leggett.*

Below: The Leggett House in Chestertown.

Underground Railroad. I don't recall feeling the presence of Joseph when we went inside that day, but we did find his portrait, of which I took a photo.

Craig also gave me an old black-and-white photo of the house that looked to be from about 1950 or earlier. While he wasn't able to provide any stories I hadn't already heard, we did find an artifact: a dead ringer for a North Star quilt. Yes, a quilt. Before you start, I should say that I know all the caveats now. At the time, *Hidden in Plain View* had recently been published, and although I hadn't read it to realize that it was full of errors, I was as gullible as anyone to believe such an implausible story. Finding something tangible at the Leggett House made me feel that I had a productive day. There was, however, another interesting bit of ephemera we found: a receipt for services for Joseph Leggett from Dr. Hiram McNutt. While it didn't mean anything to Craig, I thought it might be the answer to why two houses in Warren County had Underground Railroad associations.

If you recall, my original story about the Underground Railroad in the *Post-Star* reported that Village Historian Mabel Tucker said that a tunnel led from a chiropractor's house on 130 Main to the Senior Center. Well, I checked the history of the house in the *Warren County Book of Deeds* and found that the owner of the chiropractor's house was Dr. Hiram McNutt, who purchased the property in 1849.[53]

Even more interesting, I found that McNutt was the owner of another house in Glens Falls with an Underground Railroad legend attached. This house was on 12 Bacon Street. It was a rental property owned by a Sue Atkinson, who said that a hidden room had been discovered in the house. However, despite several attempts to gain access to the house to see this room, I never saw it. I was able to see the blocked-off entrance to the alleged tunnel in the basement of the Warrensburg house. There were more circumstantial clues though. McNutt was a Quaker and president of the Warren County Medical Society in 1863, as well as a delegate to the state medical society, of which Hiram Corliss was a member.[54] That both houses McNutt owned during the antebellum period had Underground Railroad legends and that he had associations with the foremost Underground Railroad conductors in Washington and Warren Counties seemed more than a coincidence. On the other hand, what something *seems* is not always what it *is*.

If my trip to the Leggett House only resulted in more questions than answers, I would soon find answers to a few other questions that local historians had been unable to resolve until now. The first question concerned the validity of the Samuel Boyd reminiscence in 1927. The answer to that question was a resounding yes—it really did happen. I found the story in the September 17, 1851 issue of the *Glens Falls Free Press*. You bet I reported it in my column for the *Chronicle*. For me, it was another successful demonstration that some of the old stories were true. The story reported had only minor differences from the one told by Boyd seventy-seven years later. Apparently, Van Pelt had attempted to negotiate the sale of his wife with the slaveholder, who demanded too much, and so they left town. The *Free Press* story was supportive of Van Pelt and showed the prevailing antislavery attitude of the community:

> *Here was one of our neighbors, colored, to be sure, but none the less a man for that, who had lived in this village some two years, and by his industry and good behavior, merited what he was receiving, the cordial support of our citizens. He was upright and inoffensive in all his transactions…and to all appearances, was as much entitled to a residence here with his wife, as any one of us. But by the law of the Union, in the face of the idea that "all men are created free and equal," he had been compelled to flee to the Queen's dominions.*[55]

This incident occurred one year after the passage of the Fugitive Slave Law of 1850, a much stronger law than the previous one. It gave power to specially designated local judges to remand the accused over to anyone who showed proof of ownership, prohibited testimony from the accused, required all citizens to aid in the recapture of fugitives from slavery and increased the penalties for violating the law from $500 to $1,000 for each fugitive from slavery assisted (more than $20,000 in today's currency). Many attempts by slaveholders to retrieve their slaves were made after the passage of the law, with the year 1851 seeing the largest number of successful attempts.[56] This contradicts the notion of more recent interpretations of the Underground Railroad that slaveholders would never come north for their slaves, especially not as far north as the Adirondacks in upstate New York.

Another question I answered during this time was whether black minister and mason Reverend George Brown was the creator of the Stone Chair. The artifact, which was in Washington County, was also claimed by Warren County because it was so close to the border between them. Of course, I didn't find the answers in either county but rather at the state library in Albany.

The answer was found in Brown's journal. If we examine his life more closely through the pages of his journal, we find it highly unlikely that Brown ever engaged in the Underground Railroad or created the Stone Chair.

The Stone Chair as it looks today, with the modern sign erected by Paul Loding, town historian.

Brown went to Africa for the first time in 1836, the first of three missions to Africa as a representative of the colonization movement. Most abolitionists, especially black abolitionists, strongly opposed this movement; when Brown returned in 1838 and gave colonization lectures throughout eastern and central New York, they were poorly attended, and he was heckled. About one lecture he wrote, "[B]ut for it my good Abolition friends blowed me up sky high."[57] He returned to Africa in 1839 and made another trip back home in 1841, arriving at Staten Island on July 1, so there is no doubt that he was out of the country on May 23, 1841, which is the inscription on the Stone Chair.[58] Returning home, he gave a series of lectures promoting African colonization, during which time he wrote, "Nothing is heard of in this region but Abolitionism." At one colonization lecture he gave in Vermont, he was actually attacked by an abolitionist.[59] This is not to say that colonizationists never assisted or were not sympathetic to fugitives from slavery. It does show, though, that Reverend George Brown probably did not participate in the Underground Railroad. This idea, in conjunction with his being out of the country on the date inscribed on the Stone Chair, makes it highly unlikely that he was its creator.

Meanwhile, two grants that Marilyn wrote were accepted. She had scheduled a date for the presentation, and I hadn't even started to put it together. I had become totally absorbed in the research. As any serious researcher will tell you, it can become addicting, and it's hard to pull yourself away because it seems with every new document, you have the expectation that the next find is on that next page and that it will be bigger than the last one. As is often the case, however, the big finds, like Abel Brown and the Stephen Myers broadside, come when you least expect them. Still, you never know when you will strike gold, and it keeps you going.

The search and Marilyn kept me on track. We even made a three-day visit to the AAS, which has a residence attached to its collection. It provides lodging to those awarded fellowships to do studies with the help of its collection. Usually, the AAS also has extra rooms available for the public, so we took those rooms. It was an exhausting three days of research; Marilyn has more energy than most college kids.

Yes, Marilyn is an extraordinary local historian. She was for a time president of the Association of Public Historians of New York State and almost singlehandedly put the Warren County Historical Society on the map. She moved it from a small membership without an office space when it started in 1997 to a large organization with a permanent home in a few short years. Among its many contributions have been a comprehensive study

Marilyn Van Dyke, local historian extraordinaire. *Photo by Stan Cianfarano.*

of the Battle of Lake George, for which I was a part of the team, and a new full-length history of Warren County, the first that had been written in fifty years, both projects conceived and directed by Marilyn when she was president. Now in her eighties, I talked to her recently and learned that the last president resigned and that she has installed herself as interim president until a new permanent president is found. And she sounded as vital as ever.

There were times when I wondered if I would complete the PowerPoint project as I struggled with procrastination, something I still do whenever I have a project to complete. Finally, the 154-slide presentation was done. My good friend and former colleague from Fulton-Montgomery Community College, Frank Yunker, a professor of computer science, helped me create the soundtrack. On June 23, 1999, we presented my study on the Underground Railroad in Warren County at Adirondack Community College. We received coverage in the newspapers and local TV. It was a success, and both Marilyn and I were pleased with our product. Some of the images could have been better, and in retrospect, the presentation seems a bit crude in comparison to some I've done since, but the soundtrack was pretty cool. The story climaxed with John Brown and his execution. There was a short postscript about the Civil War, and then we ended the presentation with the following words: "While Lincoln may have preserved the Union, it was a man of the Adirondacks, John Brown, who, it could be said, freed the slaves."

Chapter 7
UNDERGROUND RAILROAD
MOUNTAIN MEN

M y research seemed to be leading me north, but during the period of my collaboration with Warren County, I backtracked south. I began to explore possible connections in Saratoga. As I have said, the Underground Railroad consisted of connections along a route (though often not predetermined)[60] that led to destinations, often Canada, especially after 1850. Although Saratoga was a favorite vacation spot for slaveholders and slave catchers, the rural areas in the county were also sympathetic to fugitives from slavery, and a number of stories about aid there have survived. While the abolitionist newspapers reported on many antislavery meetings in the county, there was nothing about the Underground Railroad.

One historian suggested that I visit the Brookside Museum in Ballston Spa, which had an archive. It was like many other museums with archives, and although I was hopeful, I didn't expect to find anything. As I was going through the files, I found a typed copy of a diary written by Lydia Frances Sherman, "My Year in Washington (1848–1849)." When I started reading, I thought I was seeing things:

> *Our house was one of the stations on the "underground railroad" which ran from the slave states to the Canada border...The first station after leaving Saratoga was in Greenfield, at the house of Mason Anthony, a good Quaker Abolitionist. Friend Anthony would bring the escaped man after dark to our house in Hadley. The next night my father would take him to the house of Uncle Henry Beach, in Luzern [sic]...six miles away.*

Where did this come from? Why had no one had mentioned this to me before? I kept reading.

> *At one time we kept a fugitive about the house several days before we dared pass him along, as a reward for his capture was posted in every village and at every post office, and plenty of pro-slavery men were eager for the reward. Fortunately it happened that just at that time my married sister came home on a visit, bringing with her a young infant. They dressed the slave in woman's clothes, with a heavy veil, put in his arms a large doll, well wrapped up to look like a baby, and my mother drove with him to Grandfather Wilcox's who lived near Uncle Henry Beach.*
>
> *On their way they had to pass through the village of Luzerne, and the ten minutes spent in transit caused them much anxiety, for fear that some friend might stop to speak to them, as often happened when my mother went to visit her father. The most anxious time was when they had to go over the Sacandaga River and the North River, which were close together and were crossed by covered bridges, where they must drive slowly. Fortunately the first bridge was free, and father "commuted" for the other, so they did not have to stop to pay toll. The man reached Canada safely and afterward reported to us.*[61]

I was astonished. Why had this never been published or reported? What made it even more compelling was that it corroborated another piece of information I had picked up: the identification of Mason Anthony as a conductor. Anthony, I later found, was the president of the Saratoga Liberty Party, and Sherman's father was also a member of the Liberty Party.[62] Much more revealing was an 1838 letter I obtained from the Vermont Historical Society addressed to Anthony from a conductor in Montpelier, Vermont. The conductor told of Anthony transporting a fugitive slave:[63]

> *Dear Friend:*
>
> *I write to inform you that the lad who is indebted to your and your father's great kindness for a safe arrival at my friend R.T. Robinson's*[64] *is now sitting in my office in the State House. He wishes, first of all to return to yourself and your father's family ten thousand thanks for the generous assistance afforded him in his extremity. Providentially, I arrived at friend Robinson's only an hour after your departure; and on Saturday last took the lad (now Charles) and brought him on to Montpelier, a distance of 43*

miles. By my friend Robinson's earnest request I have assumed the office of guardian to Charles. Having no family myself, I have found a home for him for the present in an excellent family a mile from this village, when, I doubt not, he will be received as becometh abolitionists. He will enjoy the best religious instruction on the Sabbath in the Sanctuary and in the Sabbath School, and no opportunity will be lost to afford him suitable elementary instruction to prepare him to take his place in a day school. If he should make such proficiency as I have reason to hope, it is my purpose to place him in a good family, ere long, as an apprentice to the art of printing.

Yours in the cause of the slave,
C.L. Knapp

Years later, a colleague sent me the missing piece to this story that appeared in the *Emancipator and Weekly Chronicle*.[65] Charles Nelson, which was the full name of the fugitive from slavery, had come to New York from Vicksburg, Mississippi, with his master. They had spent some time in Saratoga, and from there, they were going to Niagara Falls. However, his master left him at a hotel in Schenectady, where he met the abolitionist barber R.P.G. Wright. The father of noted abolitionist minister Theodore Sedgwick Wright, leader of the New York Committee of Vigilance[66] and pastor of the Shiloh Presbyterian Church in Manhattan, the elder Wright arranged Charles's escape with Mason Anthony, who took him to Rokeby.

From Schenectady, local legends alleged that a military road (now Middleline Road) led out of Schenectady to several reported Underground Railroad stops, including the residence of noted temperance leader Edward C. Delevan, and on to Greenfield, where Mason Anthony lived. A description of a route that continued from this area toward Canada was found at the Saratoga County historian's office. It was a typed copy of notes from "Mrs. Ellsworth's Scrapbook":

In Civil War times, West Mountain was on route of the underground railway…It is said there was a station about one mile Ballston Center, near High Bridge. From there slaves taken over back road, near the Smith farm…a short distance west of M.G. up through Daniel's School District (past Frink House) through Chatfield Corners and on to Lake Desolation. From this point the route continued down Honse Creek and thru the wilderness to Black Pond, west of Corinth, thence along a blazed trail for about two miles to a little cottage owned by a negro named Fitch. His house was an oft frequented station. For a day or two the slaves would rest at the Fitch home and then be guided by their host past Lake Efnor, down the outlet to the Sacandaga River. From here they went through a section known as the Allentown, thence to Newton Farm, Hadley Hill continuing easterly for about five miles to Stony Creek and thence to a cottage near Thurman Station and on to the border.

Who was this Mr. Fitch? Through the grapevine, I was put in touch with Corinth resident Rachel Clothier, who knew about Fitch, about how he died butting heads with his pet ram, and she told me that the remnants of his crude cabin still existed in the middle of a mountain between Corinth and Sacandaga Lake—it was turned into a lake in 1929 because of frequent flooding of the river.

The story seemed too bizarre. I had to see what was there and got directions from another lady to whom Rachel referred me. The path up the mountain was a snowmobile trail, and it was one of those typical Adirondack hills between one and two thousand feet, thick with foliage and pine trees. I was not given a clear demarcation as to the location. I was told that it was most of the way up near the top and down from the trail. It had started out sunny, but gray clouds gradually began filling up the sky. When rain started falling, I was mostly under the cover of the tall trees. It turned into a downpour, and it began seeping through. It seemed to be taking longer than I expected, as is usual when you are hiking an unknown trail. Then as the trail took a slight turn to the left, I noticed a slight depression below. I noticed some rocks and a tree growing out from the middle. I stepped down carefully and then moved under an opening in the canopy of branches and felt the rain drizzle on my head. This had to be it.

The ruins showed an obvious foundation of stacked stones. I tried to wipe off the camera as I snapped some shots. Imagine someone living in such a remote place, a lot more remote than Thoreau's cabin on Walden Pond. Only a part of the foundation remained, so it was hard to say how big Fitch's place was, probably about the size of an igloo—or at least the igloos I had seen in films. Others, like Noah John Rondeau, had survived living in the Adirondack wilderness, so it was possible that Mr. Fitch lived here. According to the lore, fugitives from slavery would rest here, after which Mr. Fitch would take them down to the river, which met the upper Hudson River meandering on to Stony Creek. Farther up the Hudson, you would come to Igerna and the Military Road and then access to the Promised Land of Canada.

Martin Fish and Art Perryman at the Perry House in Igerna.

Truth, they say, is stranger than fiction, and for most clichés and legends, there is more than a kernel of truth in them. Believe it or not, I came across another "Mr. Fitch," or I should say another black Adirondack mountain man who is alleged to have aided fugitives from slavery. He was known as "Mr. Cutler." I'm not sure how I learned of him. All I can remember is that I met locals Martin Fish and Art Perryman, a retired state trooper whose wife was a teacher and I think might've been the source who alerted me to Mr. Cutler, at the Perry House.

An abandoned farmhouse, in the middle of nowhere, the home was built in 1772 and had been a stagecoach stop. They also said it was a stop on the Underground Railroad. It was a short distance from an old military road that they said went almost all the way to Ogdensburg, which sits on the St. Lawrence River just across from Canada.

Fish said that old-timer Ethan Perry, who had been born in 1900, told him of the legend of the Underground Railroad and Mr. Cutler, whom he said was a fugitive from slavery who built a barn and cabin only a few miles from the Perry House. Fugitives from slavery would stay with him, sometimes for extended periods, Fish said. I couldn't wait to see what was left of his cabin. We headed up a sloping thicket toward Ethan Mountain (pronounced "ee-tan").

Ethan Mountain.

Remnants of Mr. Cutler's cabin.

Along the way, we came across several ruins of former cabins and barns—mostly just piles of rocks, some with pieces of life-sustaining items, like a woodstove with the imprint "Glens Falls" still visible on the rusted metal. About one mile up the hill, we came to Cutler's site. Trees and shrubs had overgrown the rocks of his cabin and made them barely visible from a distance. Closing in, you could see the carefully stacked rocks that made up its foundation, much like the foundation of Mr. Fitch's cabin but in better condition. Basically a neat pile of large stones.

I wondered what could've possessed these men to come here and live out their lives. I decided to do a search. In the Troy City Directory, I found a black whitewasher named Henry Fitch who lived in Troy from 1842 to 1843 and, for a time, in 1846. U.S. Census records also show a Henry Fitch in Saratoga County between 1830 and 1840. I also found a Henry Fitch who spoke at the meeting of the "black people of the city of Troy" in May 1842.[67] The meeting was called to address the recent decision by the Supreme Court in the Prigg case. It involved the conviction of attorney Edward Prigg on the charge of kidnapping in Pennsylvania. Prigg had entered that state and taken a fugitive from slavery by force in 1837. The court had overturned the state's conviction. It stated that situations involving fugitives from slavery were under federal jurisdiction and that states had no right to interfere with the actions of slave owners or their representatives in their apprehension. Naturally, this panicked blacks, for even free blacks were prey to slave catchers, as we are all aware from the well-known story of Solomon Northup who was led from Saratoga Springs in 1842 and kidnapped into slavery. The Troy blacks resolved that the decision was "contrary to the laws of humanity and justice" and that they had "a right to resist the devil—a kidnapper."[68]

Mr. Fitch probably was not totally cut off from the outside world. Just as Thoreau lived within walking distance of his parents' home and the home of his good friend Emerson, Fitch likely found support and friendship in nearby Corinth, also within walking distance, where Liberty Party meetings were held during the 1840s and featured such prominent abolitionists as Reverend Abel Brown and "General" William L. Chaplin.

It's unlikely that Mr. Fitch knew Mr. Cutler, who could've been Benjamin Cutler, a black laborer from Albany. A member of the Albany Vigilance Committee, Cutler first appears in the Albany City Directory of 1825, listed as a man of color. Another possible relation to Mr. Cutler's identity is John Cutler, a black man who first appears in the Albany City Directory in 1852. A barber, he lists the same residence as Benjamin Cutler in 1854, is no longer designated as a man of color and has changed his name from Cutler to Cutter. At first glance, it might appear that John Cutler and John Cutter were different men. When one factors in the unusualness of the name Cutter, the fact that both were barbers and that Cutter moved into the residence of Benjamin Cutler, who also apparently made an effort to conceal his race, it seems likely that Cutler and Cutter were one and the same. Both men disappeared from the Albany City Directory after 1855, and this matches the story told by Fish, who said that Cutter came to Igerna during the years approaching the Civil War.

The stories of Mr. Fitch and Mr. Cutler seem fanciful. While thoughts of the Adirondacks conjure up an impenetrable wilderness, it actually was already quite accessible by the time of the Underground Railroad. The need to link the burgeoning market of Montreal with Albany and New York had given rise during the first decade of the nineteenth century to turnpikes that skirted the mountains. This was followed in 1823 by the opening of the Champlain Canal, which opened up the rich resources of the Adirondacks to Troy and Albany. In 1850, the year of the passage of the second Fugitive Slave Law, two railroads opened: the Ogdensburg Railroad, which ran from Burlington, Vermont, to Ogdensburg, and the Albany and Rutland Railroad, which led through Washington County into Vermont.

Chapter 8

SHALL WE WITHHOLD THIS
CUP OF COLD WATER?

Y ou can't get much closer to the Underground Railroad's proverbial Promised Land than Clinton County. On its eastern border, it's a gently rolling countryside that flattens out along the coast of Lake Champlain, a snatch of landscape with orchards reminiscent of the Finger Lakes. As you go west and south, the land gradually rises into forested foothills that lead up to the white-capped peaks of the Adirondack range like Whiteface in neighboring Essex County.

Settlers came to this region in significant numbers around the turn of the eighteenth century. Many were from New England, and some were sea captains, who also settled in other eastern New York communities, like the Columbia County village of Hudson or the Washington County town of Easton. They came to grow crops, raise livestock and engage in the lumber trade. It wasn't until later that Clinton County's maple sugar and apple orchard industries sprang up.

I was moving my search farther north after McFarland and Company accepted my proposal for a book with the stipulations that I expand my coverage beyond the Washington/Warren County area and double my word count. The basis for the history of the Underground Railroad in Clinton County to the north was similar to that of Warren County, a memoir recalled years later. However, it was much closer to the antebellum period and told by a man who actively participated in the Underground Railroad. It was told to D.S. Kellogg in 1887 by Stephen Keese Smith, a member of a Quaker community called the Union, in Peru, New York, south of

Stephen Keese Smith Farmhouse in Peru, New York.

Plattsburgh. Keese Smith was one of the leading Underground Railroad agents in Clinton County and hid fugitives from slavery in the barn behind his farmhouse. He stated:

> *Samuel Keese* [his uncle] *was the head of the depot in Peru. His son, John Keese, myself, and Wendell Lansing were actors. I had large buildings and concealed the negroes in them. I kept them, fed them. Often gave them shoes and clothing. I presume I have spent a thousand dollars for them in one way and another.*[69]

Based on today's dollars, that's more than $20,000. Conservatively, we probably could estimate the number of fugitives he aided at about two hundred. That's certainly a substantial number when one considers that he wasn't the only person aiding fugitives, and you have to put this in the perspective that it probably covered a twenty-year period, so the traffic was likely sporadic, as you might expect in an outpost like Clinton County when compared with frontlines like the Ohio River Valley and southeastern Pennsylvania.

To learn more and get some up close and personal observations, which I always have enjoyed and which has made history come alive for me, I took a trip to Plattsburgh to visit the longtime Clinton County historian Addie Shields, who had published a substantial monograph on the local Underground Railroad. She had based much of her work on the earlier research of Emily McMasters, a former curator of the Clinton County Historical Association.

Addie was a lady in her mid-eighties at the time but was as vigorous and sharp as someone twenty years younger. I had made a copy of her monograph at the state library, and she was taking me on a trip to the various locations that, legend alleged, were Underground Railroad stops. She was very professional in her manner and didn't waste time in small talk.

We were bypassing the first stop on Addie's list of Underground Railroad stops on Route 22, which runs along the old State Road, because I had already been there. In Keeseville, it's near the bridge crossing the Ausable River, which is the county line between Clinton and Essex Counties. A blue-and-yellow state marker designating it as an Underground Railroad stop is out front. At the time, no one seemed to know the source of the information, although it was believed to have been owned by a man named Bigelow. The size of the house is deceiving from the front, as it extends several stories in the back down a rocky slope to the banks of the river.

Underground Railroad authority Don Papson, who has since researched the house, said that it was owned by Asahel Arthur until 1869, who apparently was an abolitionist, judging by his support for petitions to form the Clinton County Anti-Slavery Society in 1837 and his call to end to slavery in the District of Columbia. But no documents indicating aid to fugitives from slavery have been found.

Our first stop was the Keese Smith Farmhouse, a half mile or so to the west of Route 22 along Union Road, which intersected with it. No one was home, so Addie was unable to show me the barn where the fugitives were allegedly hidden. However, I was taken there a few years later when I was invited to talk about the Underground Railroad at Clinton County Community College, and the local TV station did a brief interview with me at the farmhouse. The barn was nothing unusual, except smaller than most. The only memorable thing about it was the anecdote that when the fugitives were hidden among the bales of hay, a bull would be stationed at the entrance to discourage any unexpected guests.

Addie had interviewed Keese Smith's great-granddaughter, Virginia Burdick, whose father recalled seeing fugitives from slavery in the kitchen there: "The slaves came into the kitchen to be fed. They were chattering with the cold, and the firelight would light up their dark, startled, terrified faces."[70]

Included in Keese Smith's memoir was an account of the organizational meeting of the Clinton County Anti-Slavery Society:

> *Delegations (from the town societies at Champlain, Beekmantown, Schuyler Falls, and Peru) were to meet in the courthouse in Plattsburgh and organize a county anti-slavery society. When our procession of delegates came into Plattsburgh, we were egged and hooted and otherwise mobbed. Elder Andrew Witherspoon of the Methodists and Samuel and my grandfather, Stephen Keese, rode together at the head of the procession.*

The mob threatened the elder Keese by shouting, "Your gray hairs shall be no protection to you," and a petticoat was held out of a window on Margaret Street to ridicule the abolitionists' manhood.

> *We drove around to the Cumberland House, but were not allowed to hold our meeting in the court house. Samuel Chatterton, an officer in the army, I think, was president of this meeting. St. John, B.L. Skinner, and others spoke…nobly…from the Cumberland House steps. Skinner begged and besought the mob to desist…we adjourned to the Stone Church in Beekmantown. Messengers were sent ahead and when we got there tables were spread in abundance. The meeting was held the rest of that day and the next. The county society afterward continued to hold meetings in different towns.*[71]

Stephen Keese Smith.

As with the other counties in the lower Adirondacks, local historians were limited to memoirs like this one, as well as oral stories that had been passed down. I, on the other hand, had access to the newspaper accounts of the day, and in Clinton County, there were numerous accounts of antislavery meetings, including this one, which was published in the July 26, 1837 issue of *Friend of Man*. It was a lengthy report that consisted of extracts from a thirty-one-page pamphlet, much of which was written by Thomas B. Watson, a Peru lawyer, who was the convention's secretary:

For a number of years there have been in different parts of the county, Anti-Slavery or Abolition Societies. Within the last year, the number of town societies have increased, and the subject has excited more attention generally in this county than at any other period.[72]

Watson also reported the mobbing of the convention and the forced move to the Stone Church in Beekmantown. He included the interesting fact, not mentioned by Smith, that a petition had been circulated among Plattsburgh residents the day after the announcement of the convention, demanding that it be held elsewhere. Dated April 12, 1837, it was signed by 114 individuals. So, when the abolitionists arrived in downtown Plattsburgh on April 25, 1837, the mob came as no surprise.

Many other details were provided in the report that Smith's memoir did not contain. For instance, Watson, Reverend Edward C. Pritchett (who later became pastor of the Free Church in Union Village) and Samuel Keese were appointed to a committee to prepare a constitution and preamble. Officer elections included Noadiah Moore of Champlain as president; Silas Hubbell of Champlain, James S. Sheddon of Moorestown, Peter Weaver of Plattsburgh, Reverend Abraham Haff of Peru, R.S. Lockwood of Saranac, Dorus Martin of Ellenburgh, Baruch Beckwith of Beekmantown and Ira P. Chamberlain of Chazy as vice-presidents; Orson B. Ashmun of Champlain recording secretary; and John H. Barker of Peru as corresponding secretary. The executive committee included Samuel Keese of Peru, Reverend Haff and Horace Boardman of Plattsburgh. The main speakers were Moore, Watson, Pritchett, Boardman, Witherspoon and Samuel Keese.

A point of interest that corroborates Smith's memoir is that Noadiah Moore was elected president of the county society. In the memoir, Keese Smith noted, "Noadiah Moore was a philanthropist. He first came to The Union and stirred us up to work in the anti-slavery cause. His place was a station in the Underground Railroad in Champlain, about seven miles from Canada. He went with the Negroes to Canada and looked out for places for them to work."[73]

Noadiah Moore.

There were at least seven antislavery societies in the county in addition to the county society. These included three societies in Peru and one each in Keeseville, Beekmantown, Champlain and Mooers.[74] Of the three societies in Peru, one of them had an all-female membership. The report of that organization's third annual meeting, held in 1838, included this extract:

> We make this report on behalf of two hundred females of Peru and vicinity…We deem it a privilege, thus peaceably to assemble, and exercise the rights of free people, in expressing our thoughts on subject presented to this meeting, instead of sharing in the degradation and the calamity of our colored sisters, for whose special benefit the society first organized. An unalterable conviction, that liberty or despotism, must ere long gain the undisputed supremacy of this nation—the plea for freedom must become loud enough to succeed in the emancipation of the enslaved or our labors are lost. Repent or perish, is the only alternative left for this Republic.[75]

Three years later, its sixth annual meeting included this resolution:

> Shall we withhold this cup of cold water from the toil-worn slave and the panting fugitive…In the name of humanity, we answer NO! Remember that we are candidates for immortality, and let us perform our part, that at the final review, when there shall be neither servant nor master, the soul-cheering language may be applicable to us, "inasmuch as ye did it unto none of the least of these my brethren, ye did it unto me."[76]

Such a declaration implies that they were aiding fugitives from slavery in Peru. When confronted with such accounts, it's not so easy to dismiss the reality of the Underground Railroad in the Adirondack region as it is to dismiss oral history. This is why the early accounts, especially those reported as facts in newspapers, are so important to determining the truth about what really happened. Oral history is all that historians like Addie and her predecessors had to work with, which is why more work needs to be done to show where oral tradition and traceable fact correspond.

We were bypassing the next stop along Addie's route, the Townsend Addoms House, because it no longer existed, having been torn down and replaced by another house. However, it was a house with a fine oral tradition, and Addie had done considerable research on it. Apparently, it had tunnels in its basement, and the owner of the new house, Eugene Pellerin, had been careful to create a detailed diagram of them, which was included in Addie's monograph.

Addoms was a circuit rider for the Methodist Church and held meetings and Sunday school in what was a spacious wood-frame house. In 1979, Addie interviewed locals who were friends of Addoms's descendants and who were told stories about the house. Stella Hildreth Sanger, born in 1901, said that family members told her that fugitives from slavery sometimes stayed there and worked for a time. Minnie Wright Wood, born in 1910, said that she was told that "there were passages from the various cellars…[and] under a long table was a secret door that led to a dry cistern. I've heard stories of lawmen coming down the lane and whoever was sheltered getting under the table, opening a trap door and descending into the cistern"[77]

Such stories are typical of many that have come down to us about countless other possible Underground Railroad sites nationwide that have been questioned by contemporary historians, who demand that higher standards of scholarship be applied when determining evidence of Underground Railroad activity. However, this doesn't mean that such stories should be dismissed outright. For instance, one historian who subscribes to the contemporary interpretation said to me that the memoir of Stephen Keese Smith is not credible. Well, I would like to ask this historian if the accounts in *Friend of Man* are also not credible since they correspond to what Smith related.

Our journey along Route 22 took us to three more homes: a bar and restaurant; the Klondike Inn, identified by Emily McMasters as the White Pine Tea Room; and the Ira Rowlson Farmhouse. However, to this day, no other information indicating why these sites are believed to have harbored fugitives from slavery has been found.

Farther up the road is the Dawson House, a site for which Addie is the source, having lived there as a child. She points to strong circumstantial evidence. The house is only half a mile from a lot that was deeded to three black families who had been slaves of Judge Thomas Treadwell and manumitted by him in 1794.[78] Also, it is a mere nine hundred feet east from another lot, no. 16, where two log houses occupied by free "Negroes" were situated during the Underground Railroad period. It is well established that fugitives sought first the safe havens of those of their own race, so the legend that fugitives from slavery also stayed at the Dawson House, so close to these residences, may have foundation; it's also possibly wishful thinking on Addie's part.

We then drove off Route 22 down toward Lake Champlain and came to a small log house nestled in a bay along Lake Champlain. It was owned by a man named Trombley or Trombly. The name could be meaningful because an A. Trombly was a subscriber to the Liberty Party's newspaper, the *Herald of Freedom*, a short-lived newspaper published in 1844.

The Liberty Party brings us to another significant fact about Clinton County. It was the home of a vibrant Liberty Party organization. And who do you think was the head of its executive committee? Who else but Noadiah Moore. In 1845, Gerrit Smith, the leading figure in the Liberty Party, made a tour of the Adirondack region, from May 27 to June 15. His report of it was published in the *Albany Patriot*. He visited Saratoga, Glens Falls, Warrensburg, Chestertown, Keeseville, Plattsburgh and Ausable Forks.

In Keeseville, he met with "that true friend of the slave, Wendell Lansing…Here are many sincere haters of slavery." On the way to Plattsburgh, he met with Calvin Cook of Clintonville and James W. Flack of Ausable Forks. In Plattsburgh, he spoke at the courthouse in the afternoon and the Methodist church in the evening. Lamenting that there were less than half a dozen abolitionists in Plattsburgh, he was buoyed by the arrival of "that wise and steadfast friend of the slave, Noadiah Moore." He also mentioned meeting abolitionists O.B. Ashmun, Edward Moore, William G. Brown, Horace Boardman, Benjamin Ketchum, George Beckwith and Henry Hewitt. Clinton County, Smith wrote, "will probably be the first… in our state to throw off its political shackles and stand forth for the slave"[79]

How prescient this was of Smith, for in 1846, when the state election included a referendum to eliminate the $250 property qualification for black suffrage—or, to say more plainly, to give equal voting rights to black men—Clinton County had the highest pro-suffrage vote in the state. Right behind it was neighboring Essex County, and Franklin and Washington Counties were third and fourth, respectively. Warren County, its other neighbor, was one of only six of the remaining fifty-five counties in the state with pluralities of more than 50 percent, with statewide totals running nearly three to one against it.[80]

Was there an Underground Railroad in the North Country of upstate New York? I wouldn't bet against it.

Chapter 9

THE ADIRONDACKS' HIGHEST PEAK

The high peaks of the Adirondacks are hallowed ground. John Brown is buried there. Its highest peak, Mount Marcy, can be seen looming in the distance behind his tombstone. Not far from the top, Lake Tear of the Clouds gives birth to what was once a three-hundred-mile thoroughfare to freedom, the Hudson River.

It was here that John Brown came in 1848 because of Gerrit Smith's plan to give blacks free land there. I visited John Brown's final resting place about 150 years later. The grave site memorializes Brown and eleven of his men who died as result of their assault on slavery at Harpers Ferry and whose bodies were recovered and buried here with Brown. Most striking to me was his personal tombstone, which originally was his grandfather's and which Brown retrieved himself from Connecticut and brought to North Elba.

Brown had learned of the colony that had been formed in North Elba by Smith's grantees from Willis Augustus Hodges, the publisher of the *Ram's Horn* newspaper. Brown had met Hodges, a free black who had moved north from Virginia, at the newspaper's New York City office in 1847. Hodges subsequently published "Sambo's Mistakes," a satirical essay by Brown in which he posed as a black author who criticized northern blacks for their submissive response to racism.[81]

Long sympathetic to their cause, Brown found the poor North Elba black farmers huddled together in crude, dilapidated wooden shacks with stovepipes for smokestacks. They had named their colony Timbucto. Smith, one of the nation's wealthiest men and probably its foremost philanthropist, had been frustrated by the slow progress of politics and the failure of the Liberty Party to gain passage of the 1846 New York State referendum for unrestricted voting rights for black males. So, he decided to do something about it. He set aside 120,000 acres of his own land in the Adirondacks and other sections of northeastern and central New York to be parceled into 40-acre homesteads for needy, temperate black men between the ages of twenty-one and sixty. Not only would it give them a new beginning, but it would also qualify them to vote under the state property qualification for black men.

After Brown's visit, he wrote to Smith, offering his services to move there and help. "I am something of a pioneer. I grew up among the woods and wild Indians of Ohio, and am used to the climate and the way of life that your colony finds so trying. I will take one of your farms myself, clear it up and plant it, and show my colored neighbors how much work should be done; will give them work as I have occasion, look after them in all needful ways, and be a kind of father to them."[82]

A lean, frugal, self-righteous, fatalistic, Bible-spouting man, Brown had been plagued by a series of business failures and was then facing another. He showed up at Smith's mansion after several days on horseback from Springfield, Massachusetts, in great financial debt, dressed in a ragged homespun shirt, holey boots and a shabby Sunday dress jacket soiled with mud and blood. Nevertheless, his farming knowledge and passion impressed Smith.[83]

In October 1848, Brown sent barrels of pork and flour to the struggling black Adirondack farmers. Seven months later, he moved his family from Springfield, Massachusetts, to North Elba, not far from modern-day Lake Placid. Brown first rented a small house, a two-story dwelling with the second story unfinished and little more than an attic. Then, after a trip back to Springfield to tend to his failing wool business, for which he had made a disastrous business excursion to England the year before, he and his sons bought the farm that would be his eventual resting place.

At the time, this area was mostly wilderness. Lake Placid did not yet exist. You probably wouldn't expect fugitives from slavery to venture in this direction when less challenging terrain offered another means of escape. As some of the earlier examples showed, however, fugitives from slavery sometimes sought out hard-to-find places, like the cabins of Cutler and Fitch, perhaps out of fear of being caught and returned to slavery. They had some reason to fear this because, as we have seen, accounts of slave catchers come from Saratoga, Washington and Warren Counties, and another incident involving slave catchers occurred in Franklin County, north of North Elba. That incident involved one of Smith's grantees, John Thomas, who had escaped from Maryland in 1839. He fled after his wife and children were sold away from him, and with the help of the Underground Railroad, he made his way to Troy, New York, where he became one of Henry Highland Garnet's parishioners before accepting the grant of land from Smith.[84]

Apparently, Thomas's former master discovered his whereabouts in Bloomingdale, another section where Smith had granted land about fifteen miles north of Timbucto, and sent men to take him back to slavery. The locals stood by him, and Thomas armed himself in case any attempt was made to take him back. Intimidated by this, the slave catchers decided to turn back.[85]

Willis Augustus Hodges also had moved to northern New York in 1848, using funds from the sale of his newspaper to purchase land in Franklin County, New York, not far from Timbucto. Like Brown, he was an experienced farmer, having grown up on a farm in Virginia. Once Brown settled in, he was a frequent guest of Hodges's, and according to Hodges's son, fugitives from slavery were coming and going.[86] Among others who forwarded fugitives from slavery to Brown in North Elba were the MacDougall family and Phineas Norton in Elizabethtown.[87] Another local who harbored fugitives from slavery was Essex County newspaper publisher Wendell Lansing, in Wilmington, which is only about twelve miles or so from North Elba.[88]

A report made by Syracuse Underground Railroad conductor Jermaine Loguen after his visit to the Adirondacks in 1848 to enlist support for Smith's land grantees provides information about locals in the area who also would've been sympathetic to aiding fugitives from slavery. They included Jesse Gay and Alfred S. Spooner in Elizabethtown, Uriah Mihills in Keene, J. Tobey Jr. in Jay, Wendell Lansing in Wilmington, William M. Flack in Ausable Forks; the Merill family in Merillville in Franklin County and Rensselaer Bigelow in Malone.[89]

Unfortunately, Gerrit Smith's land was poorly suited for food crops. Even for experienced farmers like Brown and Hodges, working the land there was difficult. Although Hodges and Brown did their best, many of the grantees gave up their land. The thin soil, the short growing season and the harsh winters were too daunting. The Gerrit Smith Land Grant scheme turned out to be a failure, and the colony of Timbucto disappeared. In fact, only about two hundred individuals actually attempted to settle on these homesteads.

In 1852, John Brown left the Adirondacks. He returned with his family in 1855 and, shortly afterward, went to Kansas to join his sons. Following his well-publicized role in the battles there, he never remained long in one place for the rest of his life, although he made visits to his wife and younger children in North Elba. He sensed that his destiny was at hand and prepared himself to face it. In April 1857, he went to Torrington, Connecticut, to retrieve the tombstone of his grandfather, whom he had long venerated for his service in the American Revolution. He wanted the tombstone placed at his own grave. Steamboat operator James Allen of Westport, New York, remembered transporting the stone when it arrived at his wharf on Lake Champlain. Brown took it to a stonecutter and had the name of his son Frederick, who died in the Kansas conflict, inscribed on the reverse. He then took it with him to North Elba, his first trip home since leaving for Kansas in 1855. He placed it on his porch when he left again two weeks later.[90]

Brown spent the next two years raising money and gathering men for his final assault on slavery, which took place at Harpers Ferry, Virginia. In July 1859, he rented a farm in Maryland about five miles from Harpers Ferry under the name of Isaac Smith. Here his band of men waited for the moment to strike. Joining them from North Elba were his sixteen-year-old daughter, Annie, and his daughter-in-law Martha, Oliver's wife, to minister to their domestic needs.

The day of the raid was described as very solemn and passed with readings from scripture and a review of their assignments. One of Brown's last instructions before setting out on the night of October 16, 1859, was to spare lives if at all possible. They entered Harpers Ferry, a distance of about five miles, with eighteen men, determined to begin the grandest scheme in the history of the Underground Railroad: not merely to set a few slaves free but to end slavery itself. Three of his men, including his son Owen, had been left at the Kennedy farm in charge of their store of weapons and supplies. Taking control of Harpers Ferry was relatively easy while its citizens slept. Only two watchmen were on guard, and cutting the telegraph lines effectively prevented communication with outside authorities. As a result, Brown had the town and the armory under his complete control for about twelve hours. He had taken more than thirty hostages, including Colonel Lewis Washington, a relative of President George Washington, and could easily have commandeered a load of weapons and left the scene with a great victory. Instead he chose to stay, perhaps because he had decided that martyrdom was best for him.[91]

When federal troops finally arrived, there was no question as to the outcome. After Brown refused an offer to surrender, they stormed the engine house and captured Brown and the remainder of his men still alive. Two of his sons died. Owen, who had remained at the Kennedy farm, was able to escape and died in California in 1891. Of Brown's men, ten were killed, seven were executed and five escaped.

Although the raid was a failure, Brown turned it into a great moral victory. Severely injured during the storming of the engine house, Brown was still recovering during his trial. It was in this spotlight, in another ironic turn, that he altered the course of history. Brought to the courtroom on a cot, he managed to rise up and deliver several brilliant monologues, which were widely publicized. Among his most memorable words were the following:

> *Now, if it is deemed necessary that I should forfeit my life for the furtherance of the ends of justice, and mingle my blood further with the blood of my children, and with the blood of millions in this slave country whose rights are disregarded by wicked, cruel and unjust enactments…Let it be done.*[92]

At the hour of Brown's death, church bells tolled throughout the North. Public prayer meetings and speeches praising him were held in all the centers of abolitionism and Republicanism. In Albany, there was a one-hundred-gun salute. At the Free Church in Union Village, Washington County, there was a public indignation meeting. In Glens Falls, Warren County, the bell at the Universalist Church tolled.[93]

John Brown's body was delivered to his wife, Mary, by an army escort. It had been his intention to be buried at the site of the Adirondacks' highest peak. From Virginia, the body was taken by train to Philadelphia. A large crowd had gathered at the train station, and fearing that the body might be stolen, authorities used an empty coffin to draw people away. Then they secretly loaded the coffin with Brown's body onto a boat for New York City. There his body was transferred into another coffin, and Mary Brown and her escorts, among them the noted Boston abolitionist Wendell Phillips, began the procession northward.

The farther north they proceeded, the greater the hero was John Brown. Passing through the northern villages, solemn drums beat, church bells tolled and people gathered. From Troy, they went by railroad through Washington County on Monday, passed from Eagle Bridge to Salem and on to Rutland, Vermont, where they spent the night. On to Vergennes, they traveled by coach to McNeil's Ferry and back across Lake Champlain to Westport, New

John Brown's tombstone.

York. The remainder of the journey was by carriage. The procession stopped overnight at Elizabethtown, where an honor guard stood watch over the coffin at the village courthouse. The long last leg of the trip to North Elba was up steep mountain roads in sleet and rain.[94]

On December 8, 1859—a cold, bleak, damp day—John Brown was laid to rest. In his eulogy, Phillips said that Brown "has loosened the roots of the slave system; it only breathes—it does not live—hereafter."[95] From that day forward, the Adirondacks' highest peak has been John Brown's soul. It will continue to march on so long as there are people fighting for freedom, justice and equality.

Chapter 10

ON FREEDOM'S DOORSTEP

I f you were a fugitive from slavery and got as far as Malone, Franklin County, a mere ten miles from the Canadian border, you'd probably feel pretty safe. And if you got to Canada, you were home free, in the Promised Land, and no one could take away your freedom. Slavery had been outlawed in Canada since 1834, and it welcomed fugitives from slavery even before that. Attempts by the United States to extradite fugitives from slavery from Canada who were accused of crimes universally met with failure.[96]

Legends exist about the Underground Railroad in Malone. The tradition of its First Congregational Church alleges that it harbored fugitives from slavery in its spacious basement, which was connected to a tunnel that led to other locations in the village's business section. I had seen an article in the *Plattsburgh Republican* from 1987 that grabbed my interest, and after a long journey from Schenectady, I headed directly to the church to see if I could learn more.[97]

I was welcomed inside but was told that the church had no specific documents, letters or evidence of its aid to fugitives from slavery; it was simply oral tradition. I also was told that the current church was not the one from the antebellum period. However, its legendary tunnel in the basement that may have harbored fugitives from slavery remained. The staff agreed to take me down to take a look.

I was disappointed that they couldn't tell me more. They did allow me to review some of the church history. As they said, there was nothing specific about the Underground Railroad, but I did learn that its first pastor, Ashbel

Malone Congregational Church basement.

Parmalee, was mentored by the nation's first prominent black preacher, Lemuel Haynes. Although Parmalee did not agree with slavery, he was a zealous colonizationist.

I touched earlier on the issue of colonization when I discussed the preacher Reverend George Brown. To most abolitionists, colonization was anathema. The American Colonization Society was formed in 1816 by southern leaders who desired to send both free and enslaved blacks to Africa to form their own nation. Their reasoning was that American blacks would have the freedom to form a life on their own terms without the legacy of slavery hindering them. Portraying itself as an antislavery organization, its founders included Presidents Thomas Jefferson, James Madison and James Monroe, Chief Justice John Marshall, Senator Henry Clay and Francis Scott Key.[98] It seemed like a good plan. However, it ignored the wishes of the people it claimed to be helping. Most free blacks in the United States considered America, not Africa, their homeland. Black leaders later charged that the colonization society's propaganda served to increase racial discrimination because it stressed that the poverty and ignorance of free blacks in America was the result of their natural inferiority; this exposed their racist intentions. This wasn't readily apparent to whites in the North at first because of the professed benevolence of the colonization society and the support it received from religious institutions. In fact, many who later embraced immediate emancipation were advocates of colonization. One reason it gained so many adherents was because of the separation between the races, which prevented whites from knowing the true wishes of blacks.[99]

Does Parmalee's support of colonization mean that he wouldn't help a fugitive from slavery? Probably not, but even if he did not, a new pastor took over in 1845.

I also visited the Franklin County Historical Society and found that the story of tunnels had some credence, at least in that they existed. In 1974, an underground room was found by workers during construction at the Malone Junior High. It had walls of heavy slab stone construction and was completely sealed, without any sign of a door. It measured six feet by twelve feet and was eight feet high, with an arched brick roof. The floor was four feet beneath the surface of the ground. Another tunnel was claimed to have led from the Harison House, which was across the street from the residence of Reverend Parmalee, to another station at Coolidge Court. Some believe that it led all the way to the present site of the armory on Main Street, the former site of Foote's Tavern, which would've passed near the underground room. Unfortunately, the room was demolished when a new wing was constructed for the school.[100] All this talk of tunnels means nothing, however, without more evidence because they could've had other purposes.

The best source of information about Franklin County came from *Historical Sketches of Franklin County* by Frederick Seaver, published in 1918. The chapter on the Underground Railroad was only seven pages, but it had interviews with residents who lived during the antebellum period. The county's leading conductor was Jabez Parkhurst, a lawyer from Fort Covington, which is about fifteen miles from Malone. It's right on the border with Canada. A letter from Marshall Conant stated that "Mr. Parkhurst was an ardent abolitionist, and many a runaway was harbored and fed at his home." David Streeter, who lived on the same street as Parkhurst as a boy, said that "wagons often rumbled past…late at night," and he was told that it was "a train moving on the Underground Railroad." A third source, a letter from a Mr. Cheney, claimed that Parkhurst, Daniel Noble and Cheney's father were the three principal abolitionists in Fort Covington.[101]

I was able to corroborate Parkhurst's abolitionist credentials in the antislavery newspapers. He was active in antislavery meetings from at least as early as 1837, when he attended the organizational meeting of the St. Lawrence County society.[102] He also was part of an important regional

Jabez Parkhurst House in Fort Covington.

Major Dimick House in the nineteenth century, Franklin County. *Courtesy Debra Manor.*

Don and Vivian Papson, founders of the North Country Underground Railroad Historical Association in northern New York, perform at the Dimick House.

meeting of the state society in Albany in February 1838.[103] He was president of the Franklin County Anti-Slavery Society and a vice-president of the state society.[104] From the inception of the Liberty Party, he was a strong supporter and ran for Supreme Court justice and Congress on its ticket in 1846. In 1847, he participated at a meeting in Union Village with Noadiah Moore that named him and Moore as Liberty Party candidates for the state Supreme Court that year.[105]

I also learned that his house still existed, so naturally I went to take a look. I found the house boarded up and for sale. It looked like it might be in jeopardy of being torn down.[106] On the way there, I checked out another house that was a stop, according to Seaver. The Major Dimick House was along Route 37, the main road between Malone and Fort Covington. It was owned at the time by Debbie Manor, a widow who also was trying to sell. She was very cordial and invited me in, supplying me with an old photo of the house.

According to Seaver, Dimick "was not only an extreme anti-slavery man, but a militant one as well." Mrs. Charles Fury told Seaver that she recalled that the Major would hide fugitives from slavery in his cellar and then take them in his lumber wagon to Canada at midnight. Asahel Beebe told Seaver that he had heard Dimick talk about some of his experiences conducting fugitives from slavery.[107]

I kept in touch with Debbie, and some years later, I stayed over when I gave a presentation for the Franklin County Historical Society's summer lecture series. I got a close look at the house's alleged hiding place in the basement, an old hearth that had a small entrance that I could barely fit through. Being much smaller than average, I had to wonder how many fugitives from slavery would be able to fit through its entrance.

St. Lawrence County

In 1850, the Northern Ogdensburg Railroad opened, connecting Rouses Point with Ogdensburg. It crossed the top of the state just north of the Adirondacks, likely similar to the route that a fugitive from slavery was reported to have taken in 1837. In 1838, Ogdensburg was one of eight cities in upstate New York that state antislavery secretary William L. Chaplin urged to form vigilance committees.[108]

This reference suggests that significant antislavery sentiment existed in St. Lawrence County, the one county in the Adirondacks that I had not yet visited. It had been nearly untouched by slavery and was practically devoid of black residents persons during the antebellum period. For example, the 1810 census showed only five slaves in the county and the 1820 census eight. Moreover, the largest total of blacks in the county during the antebellum period was sixty in 1830. A largely rural county, its view of the slavery question was almost entirely influenced by the position of its churches. Settled later than the other counties, it was fertile ground for the Wesleyan-Methodist Church, which broke away in 1843 from the parent Methodist Church on account of its refusal to condemn slavery. Many of the denomination's

Hulburd House in Brasher Falls.

earliest churches were established in the county, and this is significant to its relationship with the Underground Railroad because many of its ministers participated in it.[109]

Although the county was and still is sparsely populated, with vast tracts of uninhabited countryside, it is alleged to have had a string of Underground Railroad stops. Naturally, it would be attractive to fugitives from slavery because it bordered Canada, and despite the lack of bridges to cross the wide St. Lawrence River, there were numerous ferries and boats available. It made me hopeful that I could uncover new and insightful information. I did indeed find a number of stories from local newspapers quoting town historians and information in some of the old county histories. Based on this, I mapped out an itinerary of houses that still existed, and very early one Sunday morning, I headed west on the New York State Thruway.

I took pictures and mapped out the locations. It's all in my book *The Underground Railroad Conductor*.[110] I can't say that I found anything of special interest, just typical stories like fugitives hidden in attics, basements and closets. One house was alleged to have had a notebook with entries referring to the Underground Railroad. I never saw the book. Another belonged to a congressman, another to a wealthy businessman and another to a minister.

Another had been a temperance tavern. Undoubtedly, the county's proximity to Canada led fugitives from slavery there, but more than ten years have passed since I made that trip. So far as I know, nothing much else has turned up. I wonder if anyone has picked up the trail and looked to see what's out there. I'm certain there's more to find.

Chapter 11
DEBUNKERS AND TRUE BELIEVERS

W e all love a good story. Who doesn't prefer the Hollywood version—the Disney fairy tale portrayal of life? The happy ending makes us feel good. It's the best of all possible worlds, the glass half full. It makes the sadness, pain and suffering that ends in our passing easier to deal with. Imagine you're a kid, and you have a hero; one day you meet that hero, and when you ask him or her for an autograph, he or she ignores you or, worse, tells you not to bother him or her. The reality of life so often fails to measure up.

This applies to history, too. It's part of our nature to embellish on the facts, to make them prettier, more astounding and larger than life— to turn them into legends that grow with the years. The romance of the Underground Railroad has made it especially prone to such fancifulness. As a result, serious historians whose requirement for documentation holds them to a higher standard have, in some cases, found the traditional story of the Underground Railroad to be suspect.

They have applied this to Wilbur Siebert, from whose work the traditional story of the Underground Railroad emerged. His 1892 findings were based primarily on thousands of responses to inquiries he made of those who participated in the Underground Railroad or their relatives and friends. These inquiries, or circulars as they were called, included a survey with seven questions:[111]

- What in your knowledge was the route of the Underground Road (names and locations of "stations" and "Station Keepers")?
- Period of activity of the "Road"?

- Method of operation of the "Road," with system of communication among the members?
- Memorable incidents (with dates, names of places and persons, as far as possible)?
- History of your own connection with the Underground Cause?
- Names and present addresses of any persons able to contribute other information on the subject?
- Short biographical sketch of yourself

As the years passed, the legend grew, and original accounts sometimes became exaggerated. The fascination with secrecy and hiding places began to overshadow the real history and the people involved. It got to the point that every old home with a crawl space began to be thought of as a stop on the Underground Railroad. Of course, Siebert never suggested such a thing.

Then along came Larry Gara, a maverick historian and teacher who had taken an interest in the Underground Railroad while a graduate student. He sensed that there was something wrong with the traditional view, especially with the decidedly white version of the story. He concocted a theory that it wasn't quite like the old-timers had said and set out to prove it. His book, *Liberty Line*, published in 1961, made four significant conclusions:

- The Underground Railroad was mainly conducted by African Americans
- The part fugitives from slavery played in their escape has been vastly underemphasized
- The number of underground railroad passengers was vastly exaggerated
- There was little organization in regard to the Underground Railroad, and the role of whites was inflated by propaganda and self-promotion[112]

Gara singled out Siebert as the culprit of this inaccurate story and claimed that Siebert had accepted the remembrances of the aged white abolitionists at face value with little scrutiny. Corresponding with his contention that the contributions of blacks had been underrepresented, Gara suggested that the book by William Still, a black conductor, had not been given as much attention as the books by white abolitionists because he placed more emphasis on the heroism of the fugitives from slavery than his white counterparts.

Gara's conclusions have since become dogma for many serious academics. Dismissal of the so-called white version of the Underground Railroad also has led to a racial focus of the Underground Railroad that differentiates between black and white participants and has, in some circles, led to discrediting the efforts of whites. The leading exponent of this effort to give proper credit to black involvement has been Charles Blockson, a black historian whose ancestor was a fugitive from slavery. The resurgence of interest in the Underground Railroad has been largely the result of his efforts, which produced several books that gave deserved recognition to black participation, and his chairing the National Park Service study that recommended a national effort to preserve and commemorate the Underground Railroad in 1995. This recommendation has led to numerous grass-roots efforts to learn about the Underground Railroad and the emergence of many new independent researchers.

While all agree that more credit needs to be given to the participation of blacks, the shift in racial focus has produced a politically correct and erroneous view of the Underground Railroad that, in some cases, subordinates the contributions of white individuals. An exponent of this racialist view is Keith Griffler in his book, *Front Line of Freedom*, published in 2003. In it, he suggests that both Siebert and the important white conductor Levi Coffin had racist views that distorted the truth about the Underground Railroad.[113] This is based more on conjecture and oversimplification than hard evidence, although both made paternalistic statements that by current standards some might consider racist. However, this racialist perspective has contributed to the claims that the story of the Underground Railroad as presented by the old white abolitionists and Siebert is more myth than fact.

The verdict is much in doubt, and the claims made by Gara and others after him, who have revised the traditional view, need more careful analysis. At the same time, the letters in the Siebert collection need to be examined under the light of historical evidence.

When I began my research, I had no preconceived ideas. I accepted the traditional view of secrecy and prearranged routes. The widely accepted belief in tunnels and hidey-holes also became part of my canon. I was unaware of the revised focus on the contributions of blacks to the Underground Railroad. The color of the individuals involved was unimportant to me; I was only concerned with what people did and getting the history right. Furthermore, for me, the Underground Railroad is not about slaves who escaped unaided; it is about people working together to help others escape to freedom. This is not to disparage the courage and accomplishments of those who obtained their freedom without aid because they deserve to be celebrated. But their triumphs do not fit the definition of the Underground Railroad: an illegal network of individuals of varying levels of organization that helped others become free.

We will probably never know exactly how many fugitives from slavery escaped to freedom. To see my analysis of the numbers, go to the appendix that I have provided at the end of the book. However, there is no doubt that it was in tens of thousands.

The contention of more recent interpreters of the Underground Railroad that there was little organization of the Underground Railroad is absolutely incorrect. Organization occurred at many levels. It could simply have been among members of a church in a small town like Union Village, or it could have had 209 members like the Boston Vigilance Committee.[114] Well-documented vigilance committees included those in Philadelphia and New York City, which during the early 1850s had three separate vigilance committees. In Chester County, Pennsylvania, a network of more than 132 agents has been identified,[115] and their collaborations are detailed in R.C. Smedley's *Underground Railroad in Chester County*. Other large vigilance committees operated in Syracuse, Detroit, Cincinnati and Chicago. These organizations communicated by letter and telegraph and used boats and trains, as well as individuals, to transport fugitives from slavery. There were literally thousands of people helping other people, and there is a mountain of evidence to support this.

One of the major realizations of this new age of Underground Railroad historians is that the Underground Railroad was not so secret. It simply was illegal, and people needed to keep a low profile or conceal their activities. This perception of secrecy is reinforced by the fact that few records of the Underground Railroad were written down and that some of the few people who did write information down destroyed their records because of the fear of retaliation (see appendix).

However, the public records of the day reveal widespread activity of agents of the Underground Railroad. Notorious and transparent in its public proclamations was the *Tocsin of Liberty*, an Albany weekly. It led other antislavery publications, like the *Western Citizen* in Chicago, to follow this practice and caused Frederick Douglass to condemn it in his autobiography, *My Bondage and My Freedom*, published in 1855, for jeopardizing the operation.[116]

Three noteworthy documents have survived that support the reality of the Underground Railroad's organization: William Still's Journal C, from which, in part, he created his epic book *The Underground Railroad: A Record of Facts*; Boston Vigilance Committee treasurer Francis Jackson's *Treasurers*

Accounts Record Book; and the two-notebook journal of New York editor Sidney Howard Gay, "Record of Fugitives 1855–."

An obstacle to finding the truth about history, and this applies not just to the Underground Railroad, is that history is often made by those who distort the truth for private gain. This was one of the points made by Larry Gara in *Liberty Line*, that the abolitionists were exaggerating their achievements in the Underground Railroad to promote their antislavery agenda and antagonize the South. In the history business, it's sometimes just a historian who is trying to promote his or her pet theory, like David Blight trying to make the Underground Railroad conform to his thesis about how the foibles of historical memory distorted the story of the Civil War.[117]

Today, we often try to evaluate events in the past by our standards today or look at everything in terms of political correctness. Neither results in accuracy or truth. Certainly, when we take the perspective of the best of all possible worlds and create idealistic myths, this can inspire us and lead us to greater achievements. However, history is about the truth, which balances our expectations and helps us avoid the mistakes of the past. When historians try to falsify history, they prevent us from learning from it.

Many of those attracted to the legend of the Underground Railroad are prone to believe in the myths that glorify its image. Such fabrications, like the story of the quilts and the overemphasis on hiding places, have tarnished its history and led many historians to subscribe to a view that the Underground Railroad was more myth than reality.

Ironically, Gara's theory that the Underground Railroad was largely a fabrication created by the promoters of antislavery has led to a different fabrication: a view of the Underground Railroad today that is suffused with the prejudices and agendas of a politically correct generation. Many historians have rejected the testimonies of those who were the eyewitnesses to history and the creators of primary documents, the gold standard for verifying history.

The task for the historian is to find these documents and learn about those who made them and their prejudices. This I have tried to do, although my own fascination with the Underground Railroad has sometimes swelled my expectations. If I have a weakness, I confess that it's because I am and will always be a true believer. That is how I began my quest and how I will end it.

Chapter 12

A KERNEL OF TRUTH

My view of the Underground Railroad has matured over the years, and I still have a lot to learn. What I have found is that most of the legends will lead you to a solid kernel of truth. That's why I never say never or totally dismiss a claim until I check it out to see if there is any merit to it.

While Larry Gara's main conclusions about the Underground Railroad can still be debated, there are other, more fantastical aspects of the Underground Railroad story that have unfortunately gained currency in popular culture. Two of them are widely considered to be part of the Underground Railroad canon, and a third, although not so widely known, owed its acceptance to Siebert, in part: the use of quilts, the use of lawn jockeys and the commonly held association with tunnels and "hidey-holes."

The bestselling book about the Underground Railroad is *Hidden in Plain View*, the book that galvanized the fascination with quilts and their use in the Underground Railroad. At least, that's what I once read, and it wouldn't surprise me. As one critic of the quilts theory has said, it has created a "cottage industry."[118]

The source for the story was the oral testimony of Ozella McDaniel, who claimed that her ancestors passed it down. According to the story, quilts were hung outside houses to indicate that that it was a safe house. The quilts also included coded messages that would aid fugitives from slavery to freedom. These quilts were allegedly created by a plantation seamstress who made a sampler quilt with different patterns that had different messages; this was conveyed by the knotting, stitching, colors and fabrics, all of which provided information about escape routes and safe houses. Fugitives used the sampler to memorize each one. The problem with this story is that it doesn't appear anywhere among the thousands of stories, memoirs and histories of the Underground Railroad—not one! It belies common sense that such a colorful story was never reported before.

Another problem is that the story has wooed the imagination of the teachers who wish to introduce the Underground Railroad to children. Its charm makes it an excellent vehicle to tell the story, much like George Washington's apocryphal cherry tree. Consequently, it has secured a spot in numerous grade school curriculums, spawned organizations of devoted quilters and inspired numerous children's books. As Orwell and other commentators on the use of language and truth have pointed out, if you say something often enough, even if it's false, it becomes true in the view of society. One clear example of this that applies to our study of antislavery was the notion that blacks were inferior. This was widely disseminated to support the use of slavery, and because it was repeated over and over, it became the prevailing though erroneous view, one that took centuries to dispel. Sadly, this widely held belief in quilts and their use in the Underground Railroad is based on a complete fabrication.

The lawn jockey that designated a location as a safe house is another story that has gained some popularity. In 2009, I was part of a panel at the National Park Service annual Network to Freedom conference exploring the myths and realities of the Underground Railroad. One of the panelists, Kate Clifford Larson, critiqued the story, and I subsequently followed up with a story that appeared in the publication *Antique Trader*. What I'm going to share here is a combination of Larson's lecture and interviews I did for my article.

The tale actually goes back to George Washington. According to it, a twelve-year-old slave boy, Jocko, held the horses of Washington's army when it crossed the Delaware River on December 24, 1776. Allegedly, Jocko froze to death, and Washington erected a statue outside Mount Vernon in his honor. Charles Blockson, who has promoted the story of lawn jockeys being used in the Underground Railroad, got it from Earl Koger, who published a pamphlet in 1963, *The Legend of Jocko: The Boy Who Inspired George Washington*. Koger said that his mother told him the story. She had heard the tale from Koger's late father, a former slave who died when the younger Koger was just three years old.

David Pilgrim, curator of the Jim Crow Museum of Racist Memorabilia at Ferris State University in Big Rapids, Michigan, told me that he received a letter from Mount Vernon librarian Ellen McCallister Clark that stated, "Neither a person by the name of Jocko Graves, nor the account of any person freezing to death while holding Washington's horses has been found in any of the extensive records of the period."

The fact is, though, that cast-iron statues modeled on this alleged statue were used as hitching posts on Southern plantations from at least as early as the beginning of the Civil War. Paul Casey, who has researched their history, has an illustration of a black lawn jockey dating from 1860 that is in the collection of the Henry Ford Museum in Dearborn, Michigan. Ann Chandler Howell, author of several books about African American history, researched the cast-iron industry of the nineteenth century for twenty years and agrees that the earliest hitching post–type lawn jockeys were created around 1860. This is supported by Carol Grissom in her book *Zinc Sculpture in America: 1850–1950*, in which she wrote that the earliest such hitching post was based on a model created by the sculptor Franklin Porteus Holcomb between 1855 and 1862. This apparently is not based on a statue that Washington had in front of Mount Vernon. This original model was cast by the Robert Wood and Perot foundry.

In tracing the story of its use in the Underground Railroad, the *Springfield News-Sun* reported in 1949 the claims of the Piatt family in West Liberty, Ohio, that the lawn jockey in front of their house was used to identify their home as part of the Underground Railroad. This lawn jockey is the same model as the one held by the Henry Ford Museum. This is where Wilbur Siebert's role in creating the myth originated. In 1951, Siebert's last book, *The Mysteries of Ohio's Underground Railroads*, used this story as the basis for claiming that a lawn jockey was used to indicate that the Piatt House was a safe house.[119] Larson's research, however, had found that Siebert's early research had indicated that the Piatts had not been involved in the Underground Railroad and that they actually had once tried to hinder the escape of a fugitive from slavery. She suggested that this story was an example of how people attempt to reinvent history in order to dissociate them from regrettable episodes from the past. The point here, though, is that while this story does not intersect with Koger's story, it did give legitimacy to it.

What should we make of this? Probably that it comes down to common sense. Often those attracted to the legend of the Underground Railroad are prone to believe in myths that glorify its image. Even if such a hitching post statue had been created as early as 1855, would you put such a statue outside your house to announce that it was safe house for fugitives from slavery? I think you would want to be more discreet. Such fabrications have tarnished the history of the Underground Railroad and have led many mainstream historians to subscribe to a view that the Underground Railroad was more myth than reality.

One of the most common reports I've come across during my years of research is the claim of tunnels and hidden rooms. Unlike the other two apochrypha just described, tunnels and hidden rooms did exist. The questions that need to be considered are how common they were and who needed them. In 1993, a study was published in *Ohio History* that examined seventeen houses in Ohio alleged to have used tunnels or subterranean rooms for the Underground Railroad.[120] Not one showed conclusive evidence of such use: four were found to be constructed after the antebellum period; three had cisterns; two no longer existed; one claimed that Harriet Tubman was harbored there even though Tubman never went through Ohio; and all but one of the rest had some structural anomaly that made a tunnel doubtful. The house that was not ruled out for structural reasons, the Augustus Taylor House in Loudonville, Ohio, was dismissed because Taylor was not among Siebert's list of abolitionists.

While ruling out the house because Siebert didn't identify Taylor as an abolitionist is strong circumstantial evidence, I wouldn't reject it out of hand. Although Siebert's most exhaustive research was in Ohio, it doesn't mean that he didn't miss someone. So, it would be better to err on the side of caution and leave this house open to question. However, it seemed to me that the authors initiated this study with a mind to debunk the use of tunnels and weren't open to other possibilities. While I believe that they are on the right track, the law of the self-fulfilling prophecy will always color results and decrease the objectivity of someone's research. Larry Gara's *Liberty Line* is a perfect example of this.

There are two statements that the Ohio researchers made in the report of their study that indicate their bias. The first is as follows:

> *The accounts left by both agents and fugitives involved with the underground railroad show that while discretion needed to be practiced, especially after the Fugitive Slave Act of 1850, which gave increased sanction to the searching of premises, there was seldom excessive preoccupation with secrecy on the part of the abolitionists who were involved, and little or no concern to construct special hideaways for the fugitives.*[121]

I find it revealing that they talk about "increased sanction to the searching of premises" without an explanation or a reference. While the law did provide federal authorities with increased power, in many northern states they were overridden by state laws. Furthermore, I can't recall any incidents that involved suspension of the Fourth Amendment to allow the searching of someone's residence without a warrant.

The other statement goes to the heart of the very existence of the Underground Railroad and challenges its significance and accomplishments:

> *The numerous accounts of their experiences amassed in Drew's* The Refugee *and Still's* The Underground Railroad, *as well as ones found in many scattered publications, incontestably reveal not only how comparatively few slaves were assisted by the underground railroad but also how insignificant a role—if indeed any at all—secret chambers and tunnels played in their journeys to freedom.*[122]

The authors footnote William Still and parrot Larry Gara, who also pointed to Still as the source for the idea that fugitives from slavery had a great deal more independence than the traditional story, adding that Still "serves as a corrective to the exaggerated claims...made about the numbers... assisted."[123] (See the appendix for information on fugitive assistance.)

Let's review some of the alleged tunnels in upstate New York that I already have discussed and some I have not. People commonly will say that it had to be an Underground Railroad stop because tunnels led from it or because there was a tunnel to an underground room and so on and so forth.

One source told me that a tunnel exists across the street from the basement of Scoville's Jewelry in downtown Glens Falls. This alleged tunnel is only a few hundred yards away from the Boyds and other Glens Falls abolitionists. Does it exist? Maybe. Was it used in the Underground Railroad? Highly unlikely. But is it a possibility? Absolutely. Everything is possible in this best of all possible worlds. Would I bet on it, though? I don't think so.

In Union Village, it certainly is intriguing to think about the tunnel that may have connected the basements of the houses of the abolitionists on Park Street. While there is plenty of room for doubt, the fact that most of the people who lived on the block were abolitionists and that for a period in the mid-1850s slave catchers were searching there for fugitives from slavery makes it conceivable.

The tunnels in Argyle and Warrensburg are less compelling, but they are not without substance or justification. So they can't be entirely dismissed.

Another hidden space that bears scrutiny was found in Edinburgh, northern Saratoga County, on the west side of Sacandaga Lake, about ten

Entrance to hidden room in Donna Robinson's store in Edinburg.

miles from the cabin of Mr. Fitch. Donna Robinson, owner of the house, which she had turned into an antiques store, was removing shelves when she noticed an opening under the stairway that was big enough to stand in. Stories had been passed down that such a room was used to hide fugitives from slavery in the village's former post office. Upon further investigation, she found that that her store had actually been that post office of legend from 1849 to 1857 and was the home of Henry Noyes, a member of the Liberty Party.

Corroborating Edinburgh's abolitionism is the biography of Abel Brown. It reported a Liberty Party convention in Edinburgh datelined, September 10, 1844:

> *Indeed this is a grand Convention—a new era in Saratoga Abolitionism. The house is still full, and the audience have* [sic] *just voted unanimously to stay another hour, and hear another Liberty speaker. The friends have concluded to raise $100 to employ an anti-slavery agent to go through the county to circulate tracts, papers, petitions, etc. and to lecture and wake up the people to the interests of Liberty. We have called another Convention, to meet in Corinth, week after next. Liberty is progressing.*[124]

Tyrell House in northern Warren County.

Another Saratoga County residence, on Middleline Road in the town of Ballston, was reported have a hidden space under the stairway similar to the one in Edinburgh. Former town historian Kathy Briaddy described the room as about five feet high in an area three feet by five feet and posted an Underground Railroad marker in front of the residence, which was the home of Dr. Samuel Davis. Ironically, in her *A History of Ballston*, Briaddy wrote that Davis owned slaves.[125] While this seems to be paradoxical, this corresponds to other accounts of slaveholders' homes later becoming Underground Railroad stops. Two others in the Adirondack region are the Gansevoort mansion in northeast Saratoga County and the Deridder homestead in the north section of the town of Easton. However, all evidence is purely oral tradition.

Other tunnels that have no proven connection to the Underground Railroad include one in Kingsbury, which connected the Doubleday House, the site of the Guideboard sign, with other homes on Vaughn Road; a tunnel in the village of Cambridge, south of Greenwich, leading from one house to another on East Main Street; and a tunnel in Greenfield, Saratoga County, leading from the Wayside Inn across Locust Grove to the house opposite it. Hidden rooms and tunnels alone should not be used to conclude that a house was a stop on the Underground Railroad. These tunnels, if indeed they do exist, could've been used for many other reasons, whether it be as cisterns or hiding places from Native Americans.

One other alleged hiding place that intrigued me more than any other was one in northern Warren County in a house overlooking Route 9. During an excavation of the house, a hidden room was discovered that could be reached only by way of a crawl space outside. Inside, they found tin lanterns the size of a cup with handles and a floor that opened to a separate cellar. In this separate cellar, they found a room with a Bible, a candle, a cot, a washstand, a blanket, a folded sheet, a water pitcher and a dresser. It was later learned that it had been the home of a Judge Tyrell, who met with Gerrit Smith when he toured the Adirondacks in 1845.

For an Underground Railroad researcher/true believer to see such a room would be a once-in-a-lifetime event. Of course, the room was not preserved, nor was a photo taken. So, we can only speculate about its use or even its existence. Hidden rooms, tunnels and their ilk are merely the ornaments and trimmings of the Underground Railroad. They mean nothing and were, for the most part, unnecessary and only used when circumstances required it. Certainly, no one questions the need for the room John Rankin of Ripley, Ohio, had hidden under the floor of his barn, especially not when his home was across the river from Kentucky and his sons were once engaged in a shootout with slave catchers.

Chapter 13

WAS YOUR HOUSE A STOP ON THE UNDERGROUND RAILROAD?

I've come across my share of claims about the possibility of Underground Railroad activity that had little credibility, and those making them are usually sincere. Who wouldn't want to learn that the crawl space or closed-off room in their old house was a hiding place for those seeking freedom or that their relatives were among those who had been part of a movement that was one of history's supreme acts of charity? However, there are many explanations for these hidey-holes that rule out the Underground Railroad, and the likelihood that they were used for this purpose is exceedingly small.

When trying to determine if a house was part of the Underground Railroad, the first caveat is caution. Street names and numbers sometimes change, like that of the Albany Vigilance Committee office of Stephen Myers. The house at the corresponding address in the 1856 broadside is indeed an old house, but because of the change in the street numbers, it is not the actual house. Often this can be difficult to determine. Another caveat is to be aware of the seductive power of legend. These stories are often presented as fact, and while they may and often do have substance, they must be taken with the proverbial grain of salt.

Keeping in mind these caveats, I've established some criteria based on those created by historian Judy Wellman and which Peter Michael of the *Underground Railroad Free Press* has dubbed the "Wellman Scale." I've designated five, ranked in order of significance, with seven sub-criteria.

- The first criterion is a contemporary account. The most reliable documents are first-person accounts that reveal participation, like letters or diaries. Sometimes, these identify other conductors, like one written by Fayette Shipherd, then living in Troy in 1840, to a Vermont conductor (see the third chapter). Sub-criteria include third-person accounts like newspaper reports or an annual report of a vigilance committee, like the September 9, 1840 report of a meeting in Union Village in the third chapter that reported the expected arrival of a fugitive from slavery and included a name of a person. Another sub-criterion would be an account by the relative or friend of the participant who lived during the time of the activity, like the diary extract from 1849 written by Lydia Frances Sherman of Hadley in Saratoga County in the seventh chapter.

- The second criterion is membership in a vigilance committee. The sole purpose of these committees was to aid fugitives from slavery, so membership implies participation in the Underground Railroad. Sub-criteria include less direct implications like membership in an antislavery society, church or political party, made more compelling by participation as an officer, board member or editor of an antislavery publication. A number of the latter were active agents or conductors. Although membership in an antislavery society does not mean participation in the Underground Railroad, if it is coupled with a local legend about the house, this makes the case more compelling. Obviously, combinations of criteria make circumstantial evidence more credible.

- The third criterion is a third-person account after the fact by someone who personally knew of another's participation or learned of it from someone who did—for example, an oral family legend, which is a sub-criterion. Many of these accounts exist. The researcher's task is to search contemporary documents for evidence that corroborates the claim. Also included under this category as a sub-criterion are genealogical records that show family associations. Not only do these associations suggest participation of individuals, which can be used as a lead for further research, but they also provide stories or references to stories about participation. This area needs more scrutiny.

- The last two and least compelling criteria are local legends, emanating from the files and reports of local historians, and house histories, which are sometimes provided with property deeds. Both are in the realm of hearsay. While they merit consideration and can be considered "possible" leads for Underground Railroad sites, their veracity is questionable and should only be taken seriously when combined with other factors. Nevertheless, like any third-person account, they provide a lead that could yield more compelling evidence.

In many ways, researching the Underground Railroad is archaeological in nature, a process of sifting through old documents and separating the seeds of truth from the cotton of forgotten information. So, don't expect it to be quick or easy. With persistence, the researcher often will be rewarded with unexpected nuggets.

Let's look at the possibilities of a house with a local legend that is questionable as well as intriguing. This house is located on 284 Lake Street along Lake Champlain in Rouses Point, New York, about a mile from the Canadian border, and it was owned by Ezra Thurber, at that time the richest man in Clinton County. Thurber was the customhouse collector at the border crossing and a devout member of the Champlain Baptist Church, whose pastor was Nathaniel Colver Sr., the father of the famed abolitionist Nathaniel Colver, who participated in the Underground Railroad in Union Village and later was a member of the Boston Vigilance Committee. This house was completed in 1818.

What important criteria can be applied to this house? Well, we might be able to loosely apply criterion number two, membership in an abolitionist church, although the Colver church was not specifically abolitionist like the Free Church in Union Village.

At face value, however, this criterion is not very strong. If we add other circumstances to it, it becomes a mystery. One circumstance is a letter, a sub-criterion of criterion number one, written by a man years later who participated in the Underground Railroad. Martin Townsend of Troy wrote to Wilbur Siebert that fugitives from slavery were sent to Rouses Point.[126] No other house in Rouses Point is associated with an Underground Railroad, which puts the focus directly on the Thurber House. However, Ezra Thurber is not named in the letter.

What makes it more intriguing is the romance surrounding it. Lifetime resident Debbie Fitts told me concerning her childhood that she recalled sections dug out in the fields behind the house that revealed remnants of

Thurber House in Rouses Point.

tunnel. Owner of the house circa 2000, Les Mathews, said that local legend identified the Thurber House as a stop and that a tunnel led from it across the Canadian border. However, as intriguing as the legend of the Thurber House is, it certainly is not proof that it was a stop on the Underground Railroad.

Another house I'd like to consider is one that one local historian claims is an example of misrepresentation. Bertie Hall in Fort Erie, Ontario, is directly across the Niagara River from the area known as Black Rock, a legendary Underground Railroad terminal where a ferry regularly took fugitives from slavery to freedom and which is mentioned in many accounts, including Ebert Pettit's book and in the writings of William Wells Brown.

The house was built in 1830 by William Forsyth Sr. According to legend, slaves entered the house through a secret underground tunnel, after which they seemed to vanish. It has since become a museum, and one of its attractions over the years is its status as an Underground Railroad stop.

Local historian Lezlie Harper Wells, whose heritage here goes back to the antebellum period, is skeptical. She said that Forsyth was engaged in the business of smuggling and that the house's "proximity to the river makes it unlikely that a tunnel ever existed because of the danger of flooding. If there

Bertie Hall in Fort Erie, Ontario.

was a tunnel, in any of these houses on this side of the border it would have been used for prohibition."

Harper Wells also claims that the museum has falsified documents, using a copy of the noted slave catcher broadside of the Boston Vigilance Committee but with the word *Boston* removed and replaced by *Niagara*. "They never interviewed the descendants before or now or care what we have to say," she said.

Let's compare Bertie Hall to the Thurber House, as they both are near border crossings where there is documented evidence of Underground Railroad activity and both have an Underground Railroad legend attached with a story about a tunnel. What is the difference? Thurber had an association with an abolitionist; Forsyth did not. No attempts have been made to officially claim that the Thurber House was an Underground Railroad stop, although its tenuous cachet is stronger. Until further evidence is shown, how can one consider the Bertie Hall to have been a stop on the Underground Railroad?

DENOUEMENT

I have always been a searcher, and that's what attracted me to the Underground Railroad: the search, the journey, the need to know more about its unfathomable mysteries. It's the metaphor of my life. It has led me across the nation to discover its truths—from dirt roads in Vermont to corn fields in Illinois, from plantations in Virginia to the sites of fugitive slave communities in Canada. I have been on the road, and I'd like to conclude this chapter of my life with one of those journeys, one that ended in a serendipitous occurrence that borders on a spiritual experience.

I had journeyed to Canandaigua, a quaint village north of the Finger Lakes in central New York, to visit the Ontario County Historical Society. According to my research, it had a run of copies of the *Tocsin of Liberty*, the publication of Abel Brown and Charles Torrey. I had seen only one hard copy of the newspaper, at Cornell University.

When I entered the society's library, I was told that a search of the archives would be required. While I waited, I talked with one of the research assistants. I told him about Abel Brown, who had died in Canandaigua. I knew the date, and he was able to locate the brief obit that was published in the local newspaper. He also said that the historical society had records of the village's cemeteries on a computer database. He suggested that perhaps he could locate the grave site of Brown. I was still waiting for the newspaper, so I thought, "Why not?" As he was searching, I learned that they were unable to find the *Tocsin*, so I turned my attention to the grave site search. I waited only a few minutes more. I was in luck. The research assistant had

Westview Cemetery in Canandaigua.

Grave of Reverend Abel Brown.

located it in a cemetery only a few blocks away. He showed me a map of it and pointed me in the approximate location.

It was a warm, sunny day, as I walked to the old West Avenue Cemetery. There were many broken and fallen headstones. Many others were unreadable or barely readable. I wondered if his was one of those broken or whose inscription had been worn away by time, as his memory almost had been. After walking through the area where his tombstone was supposed to be and not finding it, I began to think that this likely was the case or perhaps that it was even missing. I kept walking up and down the rows, crisscrossing back and forth. Suddenly, I turned and gazed at one stone standing in the middle of some others that had fallen. I thought I was seeing things. It was faint but, in the right light, readable. I could not believe the barely decipherable words I saw: "Reverend Abel Brown." There was a lot of unreadable writing below it. His name was clear enough though. I wondered if his spirit had called out to me or had led me here to find the last physical evidence of his mortal existence. I felt a rush and a chill. It was as if I had reached out across the centuries.

Since then, Brown has become known to serious students of the Underground Railroad. His biography has been reprinted by McFarland and Company, published in 2006 with the title *Abel Brown Abolitionist* and with annotations by me. Judging by sales, few have read it, so I invite you to read his story if you want to learn more about the Underground Railroad and what the people who participated in it were like. His story published in 1849 bears witness to its truth.

The Underground Railroad is probably the supreme example in our nation's history of a movement that, in the spirit of our Constitution, upholds the rights of the individual over government. Out of it came the ideas that inspired Thoreau to write his famed essay "Civil Disobedience" and that influenced the lives and work of Gandhi and Martin Luther King Jr., who believed that "an unjust law is no law at all." And it's the best example in our history of individuals acting out of a passionate belief that "all men are created equal and endowed by their creator with certain inalienable rights—life, liberty and the pursuit of happiness"—that the dictates of their conscience, of their moral prerogatives, of higher laws, take precedence over all others.

In the Underground Railroad, we have thousands of individuals acting out of selfless compassion for their fellow human beings without compensation. And these individuals who worked in the movement should not be forgotten and should be given a special place of honor in our nation's history. The Underground Railroad is about people working together to help others escape injustice. It is among the most honorable epochs in human history.

Appendix

SOME NUMBERS OF FUGITIVES FROM SLAVERY

Assisted by various groups and individuals.

Few of those involved in the Underground Railroad had any idea how many fugitives from slavery they personally assisted. Exceptions were Thomas Garrett, who actually kept count and claimed more than 2,300 (yet some reports claim as many as 2,700),[127] and Levi Coffin, who claimed to have aided about 100 per year over a span of thirty-three years.[128] Jermaine Loguen claimed to have aided 1,500 from 1851 to 1858.[129] However, few kept records, and only a handful of these survive, like William Still's journal, which listed 661 aided from 1853 to 1860;[130] Francis Jackson's *Account Book*, which listed 430 during the decade of the 1850s;[131] and Sidney Howard Gay's "Record of Fugitives 1855–," which tallied 254 in a two-year span.[132]

At least four other individuals who aided large numbers destroyed records that they had kept for fear of retribution. They were Daniel Gibbons,[133] John Hunn,[134] John Parker[135] and Robert Purvis.[136] Various newspaper accounts report significant numbers of fugitives from slavery aided by organizations: the New York Committee of Vigilance from 1835 to 1838, reporting 522;[137] the New York State Vigilance Committee from 1851 to 1853, reporting 686;[138] and the Detroit Vigilance Committee's William Lambert, who claimed that it was aiding as many as 1,600 in a single year during the 1850s.[139] Of the original New York Committee of Vigilance, which disbanded in 1846 and was reorganized into a statewide committee in 1847, Charles Ray, its longtime secretary, stated, "The old Committee in its time performed a great and glorious work. Its history, through a period of 10 years, is written in the personal liberty of two thousand of our fellow-men."[140] Ray's numbers can be supported if accounts that were reported periodically in the New York newspapers during that decade are accurate.

Nevertheless, these are only a small number of the thousands aided throughout the North. For those who claim that these figures were exaggerated, I would suggest that, in some cases, they are correct, especially when referring to individuals whose round number of one thousand seems to apply to so many agents. However, their claim that census figures for Canada—which showed significantly lower numbers of fugitives from slavery than claimed by the abolitionists—are evidence of exaggeration was invalidated by Robin Winks in his seminal study *The Blacks in Canada*. He wrote that "no accurate figures can be given for the number of fugitive slaves in the whole of the British North American provinces, or for the total number of Negroes. Many attempted to pass for white when in the Canadas, many were not enumerated, and census takers might reasonably have confused fugitive American with free American blacks, since the former often claimed the status of the latter, especially because of their misplaced fear of extradition."[141] Another factor was the transient nature of blacks in North America during this period. Finding a place to call home was not easy. In fact, most of those who went to Canada flocked back to the United States after the Civil War.

A more detailed analysis would prove revealing, but we probably will never know how many slaves escaped from slavery and found aid and comfort from the Underground Railroad. Undoubtedly, there were some who escaped by virtue of their own cunning and guile, but they were a much smaller number. Even William Wells Brown and Frederick Douglass, who escaped mostly on their own, received crucial assistance from the Underground Railroad.[142]

NOTES

PREFACE

1. Samuel Boyd, *In Days of Old Glens Falls—As I Remember It*, Glens Falls, 1927.
2. Ibid.
3. Ibid.
4. Interview with Jane Parrott, 1991.
5. The church no longer remains.
6. Thomas W. Burns, *Initial Ithacans* (Ithaca, NY: Press of the Ithaca Journal, 1904), 14.
7. Elbert C. Wixom, "The Underground Railway of the Lake Country of Western NY," Baccalaureate thesis, Cornell University, 1903, 53.
8. Emma Corinne Brown Galvin, "The Lore of the Negro in Central NY," PhD dissertation, Cornell University, 1941.
9. E.S. Esty to the *Ithaca Journal*, 1889 (no precise date given in archive).
10. Wixom, "Underground Railway," 52.

Chapter 1

11. *Pennsylvania Freeman*, "Letter from Mr. Stanton," July 11, 1839.

12. *The Liberator*, "Letter from Dr. Corliss," April 7, 1854.

13. Oren B. Wilbur, private papers, Easton, New York, courtesy of the Wilbur family.

14. Ibid.

15. *National Anti-Slavery Standard*, "Obituary," June 11, 1859.

Chapter 2

16. Larry Gara, *The Liberty Line: The Legend of the Underground Railroad* (Lexington: University of Kentucky Press, 1967), xi–xii.

17. David Blight, *Race and Reunion: The Civil War in American Memory* (Cambridge, MA: Belknap Press of Harvard University Press, 2001), 232.

18. Wilbur H. Siebert, *The Underground Railroad: From Slavery to Freedom* (New York: Macmillan, 1898), 126.

19. *The Liberator*, "Spirit of the Times—More Mobbing," January 2, 1836.

20. Reverend J.A. Smith, *Memoir of Nathaniel Colver, D.D.* (Boston: Durkee and Foxcroft, Publishers, 1873), 123–24.

21. *Emancipator*, "A Fugitive Slave," October 12, 1837.

22. *National Enquirer and Constitutional Advocate of Universal Liberty*, "Remarkable Escape," September 21, 1837.

23. *New York Evangelist*, "For the New York Evangelist," September 1837.

24. Joel Munsell, *The Annals of Albany, 1850–51*, vol. 3 (Albany, NY: Munsell, 1851), 221.

25. Fayette Shipherd to Charles Hicks, Rensselaer County, New York, November 24, 1840, available at the Vermont Historical Society.

26. *Salem Press*, "Spirit of the Washington County Press," October 24, 1850.

27. *Friend of Man*, "Communications," September 9, 1840.

28. Paul Goodman, *Of One Blood: Abolition and the Origin of Racial Equality* (Berkeley: University of California, 1998), 122.

29. *Greenwich Journal*, April 22, 1858.

30. Elisha P. Thurston, *History of Greenwich* (Salem, NY: H.D. Morris, 1876), 72.

CHAPTER 3

31. Eber M. Pettit, *Sketches in the History of the Underground Railroad…* (Fredonia, NY: W. McKinstry & Son, 1879), xiv–xv.
32. *Albany Patriot*, "Anti-Slavery Society," May 21, 1845.
33. Ernest Tilford, *United Presbyterian Church, Argyle, NY 1792–1943* (Hudson Falls, NY: Swigert Press, 1943), 8.
34. *The Liberator*, "Letter from Henry C. Wright," September 2, 1853.
35. Ernest Tilford, "Born Free," *Greenwich Journal*, April 1978.
36. Laura Penny Huslander, ed., *Washington County, New York, Poor House Accounts* (El Paso, TX: Sleeper Company, 1997).
37. Interview with Paul Loding, 1999.
38. *The Liberator*, "George Thompson in Union Village," February 28, 1851.
39. *The Liberator*, "Trip to Northern New York," March 19, 1852.

CHAPTER 4

40. Works consulted to create the opening scene from the life of Torrey were as follows: Stanley Harrold, *Subversives: Antislavery Community in Washington, D.C., 1828–1865.* (Baton Rouge: Louisiana State University Press, 2003); J.C. Lovejoy, *Memoir of Rev. Charles T. Torrey, Who Died in the Penitentiary of Maryland, Where He Was Confined for Showing Mercy to the Poor* (Boston: John P. Jewett & Company, 1847); Thomas Smallwood, *A Narrative of Thomas Smallwood, Giving an Account of His Birth—The Period He Was Held in Slavery—His Release—And Removal to Canada, Etc. Together with an Account of the Underground Railroad* (Toronto, 1851); R.C. Smedley, *History of the Underground Railroad in Chester and Neighboring Counties of Pennsylvania* (Lancaster, PA, 1883).
41. *Albany Patriot*, December 2, 1846.
42. Tom Calarco, "Abel Brown, Forgotten Abolitionist," *Homestyle* (February 1999).
43. C.S. Brown, *Memoir of Rev. Abel Brown* (Worcester, MA, 1849), 76–77.
44. *Albany Patriot*, "Death of Abel Brown," November 13 and 27, 1844.
45. Brown, *Memoir of Rev. Abel Brown*, 218.

Chapter 5

46. Frederick Douglass, *Life and Times of Frederick Douglass* (Hartford, CT: Park Publishing Company, 1881), 272.
47. C. Peter Ripley, ed., *The Black Abolitionist Papers*, vol. 4, 1847–1859 (Chapel Hill: University of North Carolina Press, 1991), 409–11.
48. [Albany, NY] *Northern Star and Freeman's Advocate*, January 2, 1843.
49. *Albany Patriot*, "Comfort and Economy for the Traveller," May 10, 1848.

Chapter 6

50. Boyd, *In Days of Old Glens Falls*.
51. Brown, *Memoir of Rev. Abel Brown*, 170.
52. *Albany Patriot*, "Gerrit Smith Anti-Slavery Tour," June 25, 1845.
53. *Warren County Book of Deeds*, no. 27, 192.
54. H.P. Smith, *History of Warren County* (Syracuse, NY: D. Mason & Company, 1885), 304.
55. *Glens Falls Free Press*, "Another Fugitive Slave Case," September 17, 1851.
56. Stanley W. Campbell, *The Slave Catchers, 1850–1860* (Chapel Hill: University of North Carolina Press, 1970), see appendix.
57. George S. Brown, *Brown's Abridged Journal, Containing a Brief Account of the Life, Trials and Travels of George S. Brown, Six Years a Missionary in Liberia* (Troy, NY: Prescott and Wilson, 1849), 63.
58. Ibid., 176–77.
59. Ibid., 181.

Chapter 7

60. As Wilbur Siebert stated, "An Underground Railroad conductor had almost always a choice between two or more routes…The underground path…formed an intricate network, and it was in no small measure because this great system converged and branched again at so many stations that it was almost impossible for slave hunters to trace their Negroes." Siebert,

Underground Railroad, 62. The unpredictability of the next destination also could hinge on the availability of agents; fugitives sometimes were forwarded with a letter of introduction to present to the next agent.

61. Lydia Frances Sherman, "My Year in Washington (1848–1849)," Brookside Museum Collection, Ballston Spa, New York.

62. *Albany Patriot*, October 14, 1846.

63. C.L. Knapp to Mason Anthony, Montpelier, Vermont, August 20, 1838, available at the Vermont Historical Society.

64. Rowland T. Robinson was a Quaker who lived in Rokeby, Vermont, not far from the New York border. He was involved in a number of documented cases involving fugitive slaves.

65. [Boston, MA] *Emancipator and Weekly Chronicle*, April 16, 1845.

66. By 1838, the New York Committee of Vigilance had aided 522 fugitives from slavery, and by 1847, when it disbanded and reformed as the New York State Vigilance Committee, it had aided about 2,000. [New York] *Mirror of Liberty*, July 1838; *New York Evangelist*, May 24, 1849.

67. *National Anti-Slavery Standard*, "Decision of the Supreme Court," May 15, 1842.

68. Ibid.

CHAPTER 8

69. Allan S. Everest, ed., *Recollections* (Plattsburgh, NY: Clinton County Historical Association, 1964), 57.

70. Addie L. Shields, *The John Townsend Addoms Homestead: Including a Study of Slavery and the Underground Railroad as It Pertains to Clinton County, N.Y.* (Plattsburgh, NY, 1981).

71. Everest, *Recollections*, 59–60.

72. *Friend of Man*, "Clinton County Convention," July 26, 1837.

73. Everest, *Recollections*, 57.

74. *Friend of Man*, "Clinton County Convention," July 26, 1837.

75. *Plattsburgh Republican*, "Report," January 20, 1838.

76. *Clinton County Whig*, "Sixth Annual Report of the Peru Female Anti-Slavery Society," January 23, 1841.

77. Shields, *John Townsend Addoms Homestead*.

78. Ibid.

79. *Albany Patriot*, "Gerrit Smith Anti-Slavery Tour," June 25, 1845.
80. Phyllis Field, *The Politics of Race in New York* (Ithaca, NY: Cornell University Press, 1982), 62; Leo H. Hirsch, "The Negro and New York, 1783 to 1865," *Journal of Negro History* (October 1931): 423.

Chapter 9

81. Stephen B. Oates, *To Purge This Land with Blood: A Biography of John Brown* (New York: Harper & Row, 1970), 59–60.
82. Edward Cotter, "John Brown in the Adirondacks," *Adirondack Life* (Summer 1972): 9
83. Edward J. Renehan, *The Secret Six: The True Tale of the Men Who Conspired with John Brown* (New York: Crown Publishers, 1995), 19–20.
84. John Thomas to Gerrit Smith, August 26, 1872, Gerrit Smith Papers, Special Collections Research Center, Syracuse University Library, Syracuse, New York.
85. Frederick Seaver, *Historical Sketches of Franklin County* (Albany, NY: Lyon, 1918), 644–45.
86. Willis Augustus Hodges, *Free Man of Color: The Autobiography of Willis Augustus Hodges* (Knoxville: University of Tennessee Press, 1982), xlvi–xlvii.
87. *Essex County Republican*, "Durand Farm, a Station of the "Underground R.R.," March 21, 1924; *Minerva Historical Society Quarterly* 12, no. 3 (October 1982).
88. *Plattsburgh Sentinel*, "The Late Wendell Lansing," May 29, 1887.
89. *Albany Patriot*, "Gerrit Smith's Land," April 26, 1848.
90. Caroline Halstead Royce, *A History of Westport, Essex County, N.Y.* (Elizabethtown, NY, 1904), 482–83.
91. Richard J. Hinton, *John Brown and His Men* (New York: Funk & Wagnalls, Revised Edition,1894), 282–314.
92. Thomas J. Fleming, "The Trial of John Brown," *American Heritage* (August 1967): 98.
93. *Sandy Hill Herald*, "A Bell Tolled," December 13, 1859; *People's Journal*, "Notice. Execution of John Brown," December 1, 1859.
94. Oates, *To Purge This Land with Blood*, 357.
95. Ibid.

CHAPTER 10

96. Alexander L. Murray, "The Extradition of Fugitive Slaves from Canada: A Re-evaluation," *Canadian Historical Review* 43, no. 4 (1962): 314.

97. Robert Whitaker, "Time Shrouds Malone's Underground Railroad," *Plattsburgh Press-Republican*, November 22, 1987.

98. Leila A. Pendleton, *A Narrative of the Negro* (Washington, D.C.: Press of R.L. Pendleton, 1912), 45.

99. Goodman, *Of One Blood*, 54–59.

100. Ray Russell, "Underground Room Found by Workers at Junior High," *Plattsburgh Press-Republican*, April 27, 1974.

101. Seaver, *Historical Sketches of Franklin County*, 645–46.

102. *Friend of Man*, "From the New York Evangelist," September 20, 1837.

103. *Friend of Man*, "Albany Anti-Slavery Convention," March 14, 1838.

104. *Friend of Man*, "List of the Officers of the New York State Anti-Slavery Society," September 23, 1840.

105. *Albany Patriot*, April 21, 1847.

106. The house has since been sold and renovated and is occupied.

107. Seaver, *Historical Sketches of Franklin County*, 647.

108. *Friend of Man*, "Vigilance Committees," April 18, 1838.

109. Among them Luther Lee, Cyrus Prindle, Lucius Matlack, Dennis Harris, Enos Putnam and Thomas Baker.

110. Tom Calarco, *The Underground Railroad Conductor* (Schenectady, NY: Travels Thru History, 2003), 92–99.

CHAPTER 11

111. Wilbur H. Siebert Collection, Ohio Historical Society, MS 116, Appendix A, 46.

112. Larry Gara, "The Underground Railroad: A Reevaluation," *Ohio Historical Quarterly* 69 (July 1960): 217–30. Gara elaborated on these conclusions in his book published the following year.

113. Keith P. Griffler. *Front Line of Freedom: African Americans and the Forging of the Underground Railroad in the Ohio Valley* (Lexington: University Press of Kentucky, 2004), 2–4, 8–10.

114. Austin Bearse, *Reminiscences of Fugitive Slave Days in Boston* (Boston: Warren Richardson, 1880), 3–6.
115. William C. Kashatus, *Just Over the Line* (West Chester, PA: Chester County Historical Society, 2002), Appendix B.
116. Frederick Douglass, *My Bondage and My Freedom* (New York: Miller, Orton, & Mulligan, 1855), 323–24.
117. Blight, *Race and Reunion*, 44–71.

CHAPTER 12

118. See Leigh Fellner's website at http://ugrrquilt.hartcottagequilts.com for a detailed analysis of the quilt phenomenon.
119. Wilbur H. Siebert, *The Mysteries of Ohio's Underground Railroads* (Columbus, OH: Long's College Book Company, 1951), 144–46.
120. Byron D. Fruehling and Robert H. Smith, "Subterranean Hideaways of the Underground Railroad in Ohio: An Architectural, Archaeological and Historical Critique of Local Traditions," *Ohio History* 102 (1993): 98–117.
121. Ibid., 116.
122. Ibid., 117.
123. Ibid., fn 56.
124. Brown, *Memoir of Rev. Abel Brown*, 198.
125. Kathy Briaddy, *Ye Olde Days: A History of Burnt-Hills-Ballston Lake* (Ballston Spa, NY: Journal Press, 1974).

CHAPTER 13

126. Martin Townsend to Wilbur Siebert, Troy, New York, September 4, 1896, Siebert Collection.

APPENDIX

127. James A. McGowan, *Station Master on the Underground Railroad: The Life and Letters of Thomas Garrett*, rev. ed. (Jefferson, NC: McFarland, 2004), 116.

128. Levi Coffin, *Reminiscences of Levi Coffin* (Cincinnati, OH: Western Tract and Supply Company, 1876), 671, 705.

129. J.W. Loguen, Reverend, *The Rev. J.W. Loguen, as a Slave and as a Freeman: A Narrative of Real Life* (Syracuse, NY: J.G.K. Truair & Company, 1859), 444.

130. B. Levitin, "The Underground Railroad in Philadelphia by William Still," student report for Wilbur Siebert seminar, no date, Siebert Collection, 19.

131. Gary L. Collison, *Shadrach Minkins: From Fugitive Slave to Citizen* (Boston: Harvard University Press, 1997), 83.

132. Sidney Howard Gay, "Record of Fugitives 1855–," Notebook 2, Sidney Howard Gay Papers, 38. Available at Columbia University Library, Rare Book and Manuscript Library, Columbia University, New York.

133. Smedley, *History of the Underground Railroad*, 57.

134. William T. Kelley, "The Underground Railroad in the Eastern Shore of Maryland and Delaware," *Friends Intelligencer* 55 (1898): 4.

135. John Parker, *His Promised Land: The Autobiography of John Parker*, ed. Stuart Seely Sprague (New York: W.W. Norton and Company, 1996), 127.

136. Charles Blockson, *The Underground Railroad in Pennsylvania* (Jacksonville, NC: Flame International, 1981), 26.

137. *The Mirror of Liberty*, July 1838, 7.

138. Benjamin Quarles, *Black Abolitionists* (New York: Oxford University Press, 1969), 154.

139. Katherine DuPre Lumpkin, "The General Plan Was Freedom: A Negro Secret Order on the Underground," *Phylon* 28, no. 1 (1967): 72; *Detroit Tribune*, "Freedom's Railway," January 17, 1886.

140. *New York Evangelist*, May 24, 1849.

141. Robin W. Winks, *The Blacks in Canada* (Montreal, QC: McGill-Queen's University Press, 1971), 235.

142. William Wells Brown, *Narrative of William W. Brown, An American Slave* (London: Charles Gilpin, 1849), 100–3; Douglass, *My Bondage and My Freedom*, 340–42.

INDEX

ABOUT THE AUTHOR

Tom Calarco is the author/editor of six books about the Underground Railroad, including *The Underground Railroad and the Adirondack Region*, for which he won the 2008 Underground Railroad Free Press award for the advancement of knowledge in Underground Railroad studies. His latest (a collaboration with Don Papson), *Secret Lives of the Underground Railroad*, uses the previously unpublished "Record of Fugitives 1855–," kept by Sidney Howard Gay to tell the story of the Underground Railroad in New York City and shows the widespread network that Gay and his associates had developed. Calarco has published more than thirty articles about the Underground Railroad in such varied publications as the *Florida Historical Quarterly*, *The Antiquarian*, *Journal of Afro American History and Genealogy*, *Adirondack Life*, *Antique Trader*, *Northeast Antiques Journal* and several local newspapers. He has presented papers at the National Park Service's Network to Freedom annual conference, the Underground Railroad Project of the Capital Region conference in Albany and the Borderlands conference in Cincinnati. He also was the keynote speaker at the first North Star Underground Railroad Project conference and has spoken at a number of colleges and historical societies. A member of the North Country Underground Railroad Historical Association based in the Adirondack region, he continues to work on developing the true history of the Underground Railroad.